What others say about *Refresh, Renew & Reposition*

"*Refresh, Renew & Reposition* is a wonderful guidebook for boards, leaders and consultants in the non-profit life plan community industry who are looking for inspiration as they embark on their "Generative Thinking" journey. This book is a must-read for all leaders who aspire to think, work, relate and live more fully as they navigate the challenges of being a contemporary leader and plan to reposition their community."

— CRAIG KIMMEL, Senior Partner, RLPS Architects

"This book is a valuable resource for anyone involved in the development or management of life plan communities. It provides advice for Board members, C-suite executives, employees and consultants about what they should consider as they manage their responsibilities. It is an easy read with lots of real-life experiences"

— RUSS ARMISTEAD, Former CEO and Board Member, University of Florida Health Jacksonville

"As we enter a period of significant increase in the number of seniors in the United States, it is critical that organizations foster a sense of urgency to meet this growing demand. *Refresh, Renew & Reposition* highlight many of the key issues providers must meet, and overcome, to successfully grow."

— TOMMY BREWER, Managing Director, Senior Living, Ziegler

"I've known the author for a long time and consider him a good friend. His passion for leadership and mentoring is truly inspiring, and this book reflects that dedication. It's a comprehensive and insightful guide to the complex but deeply rewarding process of repositioning senior living communities. With practical strategies, real-world examples, and a focus on the human aspect of leadership and service, it provides invaluable lessons for anyone involved in this mission-driven work. The author's extensive experience and unwavering commitment to improving the lives of older adults shine through, making this a must-read for current and future leaders in the senior living industry. If you're looking to make a lasting impact in your community, this book offers both inspiration and the actionable tools to succeed."

— ALEX CANDALLA, Regional VP of Operations,
Pacific Retirement Services Management Inc.

"Mark Steele's *Refresh, Renew & Reposition* is an indispensable guide for leaders in senior communities, brimming with profound insights, practical advice, and invaluable resources. This warm and compelling book equips readers to adeptly navigate the complexities of today's challenging landscape. Steele's work is a rare gem that not only inspires innovative program development but also provides examples of management and business practices to ensure financial strength and success. An absolute must-read, highly recommended!"

— DAVID TROXEL, Dementia Care Consultant and Co-Author,
The Best Friends Approach to Dementia Care

"Mark's book is a must-read for anyone navigating the complexities of leadership and strategic repositioning in the nonprofit senior living sector. His insights into financial feasibility, operational excellence, and industry innovation are invaluable. But what truly sets this book apart is Mark himself—his deep commitment to mentoring and servant leadership. I have learned so much from Mark, not only through his strategic expertise but through the way he invests in others. His generosity in sharing knowledge, his ability to guide without imposing, and his unwavering belief in the potential of those he mentors have made a lasting impact on me and so many others. I am so happy he wrote this book, and I know it will inspire and guide countless professionals in our field."

— TARA MCGUINNESS, COO, Institute on Aging

REFRESH, RENEW & REPOSITION

Strategies for Leaders of Senior Living Communities

Mark A. Steele

© 2025 by Mark A. Steele

All rights reserved. No portion of this book may be reproduced, stored in a retrieval system, or transmitted in any form or by any means—electronic, mechanical, photocopy, recording, scanning, or other—except for brief quotations in critical reviews or articles, without the prior written permission of the publisher.

Published by The Steele Consulting Group

Book design by Marty Shaughnessy / Signal Hill
Original cover image by Anamul Hasan / Adobe Stock

ISBN 9798313323862

Printed in the United States of America

TABLE OF CONTENTS

Foreword	ix
Introduction	1
PART ONE: Review the Past and Repurpose the Present	9
1. Establish Where You Are	13
2. Listen to Your Stakeholders	25
3. Repurpose Your Strategic Plan	31
PART TWO: Reposition for the Future	41
4. Repositioning Leadership	43
5. Repositioning Culture	57
6. Repositioning the Board of Directors	73
PART THREE: Renew—Making It Happen	85
7. Repositioning the Physical—A Process	87
8. The Legacy of Mentoring	99
Afterword	109
Acknowledgments	111
Appendix A	115
Appendix B	121
Appendix C	127
Appendix D	129
Appendix E	133
About the Author	147

FOREWORD

As the demographic landscape of the United States shifts with an aging population, the importance of life plan communities remains at the forefront of societal development. Today more than ever, these communities must evolve to meet the changing needs and expectations of seniors. This book is timely and essential reading for anyone involved in the planning, management, or revitalization of life plan communities. It offers a comprehensive look at how these communities can stay competitive and relevant in a rapidly changing environment.

With the Baby Boomer Generation entering retirement, the demand for high-quality life plan communities is increasing. Aging life plan communities face the challenge of not only maintaining but also enhancing their appeal to a discerning clientele. This book delves into the strategies and innovations necessary to attract and retain residents, ensuring these communities remain vibrant and desirable. It provides insights into current trends and future projections, making it a critical resource for stakeholders aiming to future-proof their establishments.

Repurposing aging life plan communities—and planning new ones—requires more than just a focus on infrastructure. It necessitates a holistic approach that considers the physical, emotional, and social well-being of residents. This book emphasizes that successful planning extends beyond bricks and mortar; it involves creating an environment that fosters community, supports health and wellness, and enhances the overall quality of life. Through detailed case studies and expert analyses, readers will learn how to implement a multifaceted approach to revitalization, ensuring their communities thrive in every aspect.

At the heart of this book is Mark Steele, a respected and trusted figure in the field of life plan community development in the United States and across the world. His extensive experience and deep understanding of the industry make him an invaluable guide. Mark's insights, drawn from years of hands-on experience and collaboration with various stakeholders, provide practical advice and strategic direction. His commitment to enhancing the lives of seniors is evident throughout the book, making it not only an informative read but also an inspiring one. Mark has been a trusted mentor and good friend to me personally, and I think his words will inspire you as they have me.

The aging demographic in the United States presents both challenges and opportunities. As people live longer, there is an increased need for communities that can support an active, healthy, and fulfilling lifestyle. This book addresses the critical issues arising from this demographic shift, such as the demand for better healthcare, the importance of social connections, and the need for adaptable living spaces. By understanding these trends, readers will be better equipped to create life plan communities that cater to the evolving needs of an aging population.

This book serves as a vital resource for anyone involved in the development or management of life plan communities. It provides timely, holistic, and practical guidance, ensuring these communities not only survive but thrive in the years to come.

Tom Akins, President and CEO
LeadingAge North Carolina
August 2024

INTRODUCTION

Two weeks after starting my new job as CEO of Salemtowne, a retirement community in Winston-Salem, North Carolina, I found myself sitting in our lawyer's office signing my name for a $42 million bond loan to pay for a new healthcare building. Built in 1972, the nursing center was showing its age. And I may have been showing some sweat.

I must admit, I was anxious about signing for such a high-dollar, board-approved project for which I had no input! *What have I gotten myself into?* I wondered. *What if this project fails?*

My wife and I had moved from California, far from our families to a place where we knew no one. Moreover, instead of shifting to cruise control at the beginning of my third decade in senior living, I was about to take on a major initiative that the board and staff had planned before I got there. Fortunately, I had room to complement their plans with some of my own experience with design construction and programs. Little did I know the journey ahead would be filled with the twists and turns, beautiful vistas, and challenging climbs that keep leaders up at night!

In addition to the new construction, I had agreed to help Salemtowne start the renewal process that all life plan and senior communities must undergo every ten to twenty years. We call this renewal process "repositioning," essential for a senior living community to remain competitive and thrive. Repositioning is a complex process that when done right advances the organization. When done incorrectly it can cause a community to go bankrupt and fail.

Throughout my tenure at Salemtowne, new projects continued. After completing the first construction project, the board approved another building project that significantly improved residents' lives and moved us into a stronger financial position. Along the way, we revamped our services and added new product lines. We embraced resident engagement by empowering the resident council. We changed our employee culture with leadership development and introduced a Ritz-Carlton approach to customer service. In addition, we worked with the board to improve governance procedures and build a stronger strategic plan.

It turned out I had signed up for quite an adventure!

* * *

Buildings are much like living organs. They need to be kept up, maintained, refreshed, and now and then "surgically repaired or in some cases removed," to keep an organization healthy. When I walked down the halls of Salemtowne's beloved healthcare center during one of my visits to interview with the board, I saw a tired building. The wear and tear on doors and walls was not even the biggest issue. The design, hearkening back to a bygone era, was predominantly rooms with two beds, only a few private rooms that didn't include personal showers, and long hallways fanning out from a central nursing station with antiquated equipment. It resembled an institutional setting rather than a modern community.

Fortunately, Salemtowne's board and previous administration had also recognized the issues. They had embarked on an audacious and courageous plan to build a new healthcare center, to start the process of repositioning Salemtowne to be more competitive and financially sound in the future.

Continuing care retirement communities, or life plan communities, number 1,911 in the United States.[1] Many of these communities have been around for more than thirty years. Newer communities promote desirable amenities on campuses with great curb appeal. While some older communities have made significant campus improvements, many have carried out only modest renovations. **So how does an older community stay competitive, especially as waves of baby boomers retire?**

The market tells us baby boomers want modern-looking apartments, bistros and high-end dining options, fitness centers, community theaters, state-of-the-art healthcare centers, and homelike memory support programs. Can an older campus be remade to meet those demands? If so, how does that happen in a place where people already live and work? And how do you pay for transformation without losing your vision, mission, and core values?

Leaders in the senior living field need a roadmap for the journey.

---

1 Dan Herman, "State of Senior Living," presentation, Zeigler 26th Annual Senior Living Finance and Strategy Conference, Orlando, FL, September 21, 2023, and https://www.seniorliving.org/statistics-about-seniors/.

After researching the process of repositioning, I found there was very little written on the subject. That inspired this book, which I've written to serve as a guide to leaders, boards, and industry service providers about how this process works. I feel compelled to document the journey for others. Why? Because repositioning is essential to sustain the mission of providing what seniors need for body, mind, and spirit as they age.

* * *

For me, the mission is why I do this work. I am passionate about caring for older adults. You could say it's in my blood.

It all started for me as a young boy watching my grandfather take care of my grandmother, blinded by glaucoma. I could see his love for her in the way he got up early in the morning to make her breakfast, leading her to a hot meal and guiding her to the table so that she would not stumble. He cheerfully did the chores around the house and read books to her that she could not read herself. The joy he experienced in helping her overcome challenges impressed me greatly. He was the other half that made her whole. I decided that one day I too would help older adults enjoy their later years.

Then, in the early 1960s, my dad, a pastor by profession, helped his Presbyterian denomination develop and build Park Shore on Lake Washington in Seattle, the first high-rise retirement community on the lake. Dad showed me that we could be creative in the design of environments for older adults. Most apartments had a beautiful view of the lake and Mount Rainier towering on the other side. The park next door offered a place to walk in good weather. This early experience began to shape my vocational vision that older adults could live in environments of beauty and purpose during their later years.

Fast forward many years, to when my parents moved into their first retirement community in the early 1990s. Dad and Mom were 74 years old at the time. Little did we know that we would lose Dad in two short years to prostate cancer. But Mom would live an additional 22 years, passing away at the age of 98!

During these years, my siblings and I helped Mom, particularly my twin sister, move through all three levels of care, from a residential apartment to an assisted living apartment, and finally, to spend the last three years of her life semi-paralyzed from a stroke in a small, two-bed skilled nursing room. Although the community took very good care of her, it broke my heart to see that mom had to share a bathroom with another person and had to be wheeled down the hall to a shower shared by all residents.

Mom depended on a staff member to get around because of her paralysis. She had a hard time sleeping at night because her roommate suffered from dementia. Despite a very kind staff, the place felt clinical, far from the home I wanted Mom to enjoy. I started thinking that there must be a better way to care for our frailest residents in a true home environment. I wished she would have permitted me to move her to Fresno, California, where my former organization had just completed a beautiful neighborhood-designed healthcare center with private rooms, personal showers, and the home amenities of a living room, dining room, and accessible cook-to-order kitchens.

Consequently, because of experiencing the continuing care model both as a career professional and as a son, I have a unique understanding of the strengths and weaknesses of the life plan community. My mom thrived as a resident when she socialized with others, swam daily, traveled, and spent time with family. But the skilled nursing experience was challenging for her as well as her children. I knew there was a better way.

* * *

Our industry has published numerous articles on the shift in models of care from clinical to home environment. But there remains a dearth of literature on the topic of renewing communities, especially on how to redevelop a campus while maintaining a consistent level of care for current residents. Without such advice, leaders must figure this out on their own or depend solely on consultants to usher them through the development process.

I hope this book will help younger leaders in the field. Ziegler, a financial services firm specializing in senior living, reports that many CEOs in life plan communities are in the baby boom cohort, and that 34 percent will retire in the next five years.[2] This means younger leaders are stepping onto campuses that, in many cases, are older than they are. They must think through how their communities can stay competitive. They need counsel on all facets of redevelopment, from financing to construction to change management.

If you are an executive, board member, or an emerging leader and

---

2   Lisa McCracken, "CEO Turnover Update," Z-News, *Senior Living Finance,* June 5, 2023.

find yourself at the crossroads of new programs and building projects, this book is for you. It's not meant to be a step-by-step manual (although I have included some helpful tools)—rather, it is an attempt to share my personal experience walking with others on the journey of repositioning. The chapters ahead will acquaint you with why repositioning is critical today, what is involved to start the process, who needs to be involved, and how to identify the tactical steps to make it happen. The book ends with one of the most important ingredients for a successful journey: mentoring. Without it, most of us would not be here.

PART ONE: REVIEW THE PAST AND REPURPOSE THE PRESENT
FIRST IMPRESSIONS

"If you don't know where you are going, you'll end up someplace else."
–Yogi Berra

After my final interview with the Salemtowne search committee, I had six hours before my flight back to California. I decided to do a little investigating while I was in North Carolina. I had met with the committee in Greensboro, so it was only a short drive to Salemtowne in Winston-Salem. Getting inside the community proved difficult. Google Maps took me to a side gate with no entry. Through the gate speaker system, I spoke to a guard who told me to drive around to the front gate. Well, that sounded simple enough. But I had to drive a confusing two miles around the community, missing the turn to the front gate. (First note to self: Change Google directions if I am offered the job!)

One benefit of my detour: I saw the neighborhood. A collection of smaller, older homes and a few apartment complexes surround Salemtowne on three sides. The homes looked like they may have been built around the mid-1980s, but they were not too far away from the stately homes built when Winston-Salem was known as a tobacco town.

I also drove by the original Moravian settlement, Bethabara, built in 1753. Here I saw the historic buildings as well as crumbling foundations where homes used to be, a village surrounded by an old fort palisade.

Finally, I arrived at the gate. A guard stepped out of the Welcome Center enclosure as I rolled down the window. I explained that I was visiting the area as a member of LeadingAge, our profession's national association. I told her I wanted to see if I could get a tour of the community, as I had heard good things about it.

The guard politely asked me a few questions about who I was and where I was from. She wrote down my license number, then lifted the gate and let me in. I drove onto the campus and headed toward the main building. I remember driving up a well-landscaped hill and passing homes adorned with Moravian arches over their front porches. As I drove past the cottages, the road went downhill and around a bend, and then I was facing an impressive brick structure called the Commons Building, connected to four floors of apartments. I parked, walked up to the front desk, and asked the receptionist if someone could give me a tour. No one was available. (Second note to self: Make sure multiple team members know how to give tours, ensuring constant availability.) So, I asked for a map and walked the campus on my own.

First, I walked down the hallway toward the main meeting room. The carpet looked a bit faded. The main meeting room, designed like the inside of a church, featured a very beautiful stained-glass window in the center, with symbols of Moravian church values. The farther I walked, down halls into different connected buildings, the more I saw significant deferred maintenance. The dining room showed signs of wear, and much of the kitchen equipment appeared to be older than other equipment I had worked with in other communities.

Walking outside, I noticed that the buildings constructed decades ago had rust stains below the windows from old AC window units. The road's blacktop surface was cracked. The campus comprises over 120 acres, including a lot of landscaping. When I visited, some of the landscaping looked well-kept while other parts needed maintenance. I also noticed that the signs were not easy to follow for newcomers.

In spite of the signs of age, the indications of Salemtowne's faith-based heritage impressed me. The symbols featured in the stained-glass windows dated back to the 1500s with the traditions of the Love Feast and the invention of the 26-pointed Moravian star. And I saw the smiles of the residents I passed. I stepped inside the chapel and looked at its beautiful stained-glass window. I felt at peace. I had a feeling I belonged here.

Clearly, there was work to do. I knew it was going to be a multiyear endeavor. Yet in my gut I felt I could help — and I got excited!

1

ESTABLISH WHERE YOU ARE
PRESENT SPEAKS TO PAST AND FUTURE

"To know thyself is the beginning of wisdom."
–Socrates

To move into a life plan community, prospective residents undergo a health assessment to determine if they can live on their own or require assistance. Years ago, my uncle balked at the assessment before he moved into Mount Miguel, a Covenant Living community in San Diego. I remember him saying, "If I can survive the Battle of the Bulge, I'll be fine in this place." But he relented, and it was determined that he needed minimal assistance, which could be provided in a residential living apartment. He moved in at the age of eighty and lived in the community for fourteen years.

Assessments apply to organizations as well. As an organization, it is important to evaluate our current state in order to determine where we are in the organizational life cycle and what assistance or changes we might need. Comparing organizations to the organic world, academics have observed that organizations, like living organisms, go through stages. They are born (established or formed), they grow and develop, they reach maturity, they begin to decline and age, and finally, in many cases, they die.

Organizational Life Cycle

The classic organizational life cycle (OLC) has five observable growth stages: Birth, growth, maturity, decline, and renewal or death. Many nonprofit senior living communities were founded by service organizations, congregations, or denominational agencies that wanted to meet the needs of their leaders or members when they retired. A growing community would add more residential living apartments, new programs and services, and additional healthcare beds; through that growth, the community would eventually expand its market beyond service and congregational leaders and members. As the community matured, the buildings and amenities would begin to look worn and in need of renewal or replacement. If the community took no action to remedy the problem, the community would begin a downward decline that could lead to its demise. But such a decline could also serve as the catalyst for renewal. Therefore, it is important for leaders to become aware of where their organization is in the life cycle so they can respond accordingly. Figure 1 is an illustration of the five phases of the organizational life cycle.[3]

---

3   John W. McCoy, "Organizational Life Cycle: Definitions, Models, and Stages," Academy to Innovate HR (AIHR) (blog), accessed January 3, 2025, https://www.aihr.com/blog/organizational-life-cycle/.

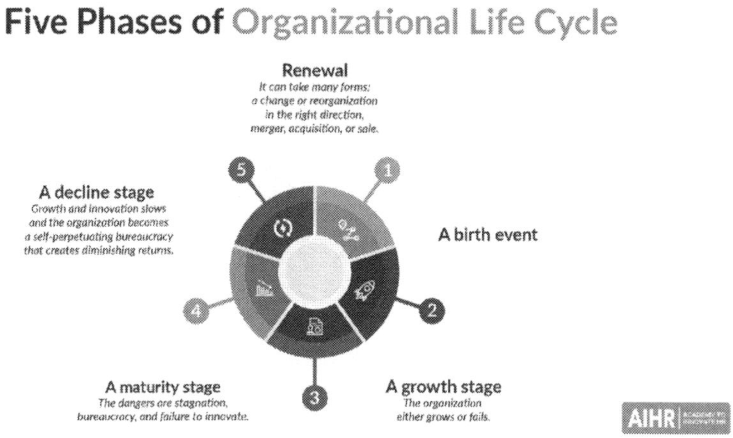

Five Phases of Organizational Life Cycle

Renewal
It can take many forms;
a change or reorganization
in the right direction,
merger, acquisition, or sale.

A decline stage
Growth and innovation slows
and the organization becomes
a self-perpetuating bureaucracy
that creates diminishing returns.

A birth event

A maturity stage
The dangers are stagnation,
bureaucracy, and failure to innovate.

A growth stage
The organization
either grows or fails.

Figure 1. The Five Phases of an Organizational Life Cycle

Life Cycle Decline

Understanding the signs of decline provides the key to using this model. The first sign in a senior living community is easy to spot—an increase in deferred maintenance. Examples include cracked asphalt, overgrown landscape, faded carpets, outdated decor, and old appliances.

The second symptom, which is harder to spot, is old technology and outdated standard operating procedures. Is the organization investing in new finance and healthcare systems? Does the organization regularly review and update its policies and procedures? Is the organization in compliance with all federal and state regulations?

Another indication of decline is the employee and resident culture. Are residents happy and engaged? Do they regularly tell others how much they like their community? How about the employee culture? Do employees smile? Do they greet visitors on campus with sincere friendliness and ask if they can help? Do they engage with others or walk by them talking on their mobile phones?

The quality of the leadership team can also signal decline. Do leaders collaborate on common goals? Or is there regular infighting and siloed behavior? Is there an attitude of abundance or a pessimistic, limited-resource mentality?

If you're honest with yourself in answering these questions, the results might demonstrate outward and inward deterioration—not always easy to spot. By understanding the five stages, leaders can assess where the community is in the life cycle and intervene as necessary to keep it growing toward a "prime" state.

Life Cycle Renewal

The concept of "prime" is part of a ten-stage OLC model conceived by Dr. Ichak Adizes.[4] Prime is not a stage in the life cycle, but the part of it between maturity and decline, a "sweet spot." At this point, organizations can stay at an optimal operating level and minimize the dips and declines. Communities in this sweet spot make it a priority to identify the signs of decline and continually set goals for improvement. The board and management work hand in glove to maintain the prime state and avoid the vulnerable position that results from decline. This also helps the community stay competitive in the marketplace.

---

4 "Lifecycle Location | Prime," Adizes Institute Worldwide, accessed January 16, 2025, https://adizes.lv/lifecycle/prime/.

Knowing when to expand facilities and being willing to take risks that lead to growth is one way organizations can stay in the prime position of the life cycle. A great example of this can be found at Glenaire Retirement Community in Cary, North Carolina. Tim Webster, currently co-president of Kintura, recounts the journey of repositioning. The vision for the community emerged in 1988 when Raleigh-area Presbyterian churches noticed a need for senior care in their congregations and opportunities in the market for additional care communities. They raised $1.7 million through donations and, with an initial budget of $3 million, started development in nearby Cary on thirty-three acres originally owned by the Dunham family.

The first phase was built in 1993 for $27 million in tax-exempt bonds approved by the North Carolina Medical Care Commission. That phase had an optimal mix of 114 residential apartments, 34 cottages, 20 assisted living apartments, and 20 skilled nursing rooms. Over the next twenty years, Glenaire invested an additional $36.2 million in multiple expansions, resulting in a campus with 212 residential apartments and free-standing homes, 49 assisted living apartments, and 71 nursing rooms, serving about 380 residents in total. By 2013, the thirty-three acres were built out. Glenaire could no longer expand, despite high market demand and a long waiting list.

At that time, three acres came available across the street. Though not enough land for expansion, Glenaire purchased the property. Then a miracle happened. Adjacent to the three acres was a former Kmart converted into a Carolina Pottery store plus a mix of commercial spaces, adding up to ten acres. A local developer called to say that he had an option on the Carolina Pottery property for a Publix grocery store and wondered if Glenaire would sell the three acres it had acquired that adjoined the Carolina Pottery? The board and management responded with a resounding "no." Months later the same developer called to say Publix chose a different site and wondered if Glenaire was interested in purchasing the Carolina Pottery? The answer again was "no," but management called the Carolina Pottery owner directly and began to work out the purchase of the property. Glenaire now had approximately thirteen acres for a major expansion to its campus.

The parcels enabled a significant $190 million expansion: A six-story building with 192 residential living apartments, 35 assisted living apartments, and an adult day care center that can accommodate up to fifty persons. The building also added multiple common space restaurants, meeting spaces, and fitness areas. Construction started in 2019 and was completed in 2024. Continuous commitment to growth led to one of the most successful repositionings in the United States, resulting in a ten-year wait list of 800 households. The new building was Glenaire's tenth expansion or major renovation in its thirty-plus-year history.

Glenaire's board, recognizing a strong market, never stopped looking for ways to buy adjacent land. Leadership at Glenaire understood that new construction wasn't the only thing needed to stay competitive. It would take twenty years to reach the full build-out. In the meanwhile, Glenaire needed to spruce up their existing facilities—in part to stay competitive with newer communities. They did this while the repositioning continued. Glenaire knew it needed to do something to stay in the prime state. Rather than accept a slow decline, leaders chose renewal. As the Glenaire story shows, repositioning is an ongoing endeavor.

Timing and Readiness

Every community must answer two important questions when assessing the organization: When should we reposition? And what leadership and other capabilities do we need to start repositioning?

To determine timing and readiness for repurposing, project consultants Tommy Brewer of Ziegler (a firm that specializes in senior living finance) and Brian Schiff of BS&A (Brian Schiff & Associates, a firm that specializes in senior services management consulting) advise communities to check four areas:

Are you meeting your mission? If the answer is no, is it because you do not have the physical facilities to do so? If the answer is yes, is there an opportunity to expand your mission and serve more older adults? Your answers will help reveal whether you need to reposition.

What is your market position? Are you the market leader or are you chasing your competition? It's crucial to know how consumers view your product and what they say about you versus your competition. Are consumers looking for something neither you nor your competition offer? Schiff often says, "We want to leap over the market and get out in front of the competition." It's prudent to continually monitor the competition and compare where your community excels and where it lacks in services and building designs.

What is your financial position? You want to reposition the community from a place of financial strength—before market factors (e.g., competition, shift in consumer sentiment, economic downturn) weaken you. Glenaire started repositioning early, when its occupancy was high, the waiting list long, and market demand growing. A community struggling with occupancy or not meeting financial targets may not be ready to reposition. Timing is everything. Brewer shares a graph visualizing the opportune moment to reposition a community.[5] As Figure 2 shows, a community never wants to get in a spot where market position and financial viability decline at the same time. To determine your financial health and how you fare against your competition, review the annual actuarial report, census trends, and the Annual Financial Ratios and Trend Analysis of the Commission on Accreditation of Rehabilitation Facilities (CARF).[6] This comprehensive publication presents comparative data for 17 financial ratios, categorized by contract type and quartile rankings, and uses Fitch credit rating categories for broader comparisons. With 28 years of historical data, it offers valuable insights into financial trends and senior living resiliency.

---

5   Tommy Brewer and Lisa McCracken, "Salemtowne Growing into the Future," presentation, Salemtowne Board Retreat, Winston-Salem, NC, January 15, 2019.
6   Patrick Heavens, "Retirement Communities a Joint Project of CARF, Ziegler and Baker Tilly," Baker Tilly, October 17, 2024, https://www.bakertilly.com/insights/2024-carf-report, accessed January 3, 2025.

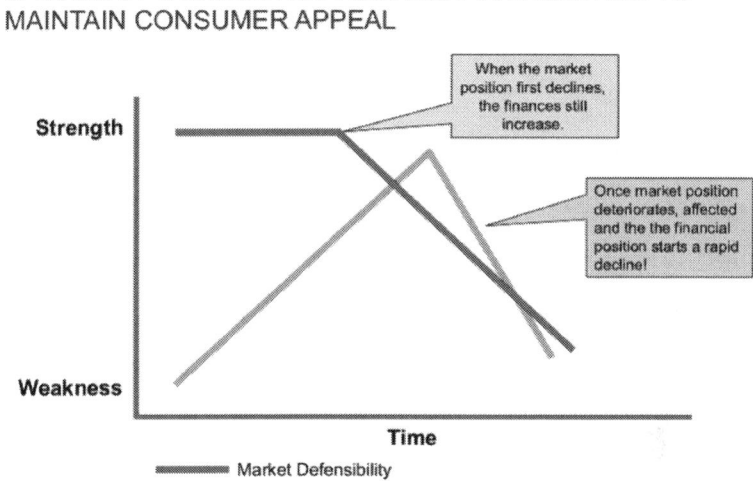

Figure 2. Ideal Timing for Repositioning

What is your management's strength? In all areas, a frank assessment is important. But this fourth question requires brutal honesty. Is your leadership capable? Are the necessary skills and experience present? Can the board and the management team develop and execute a repositioning plan? As I noted, repositioning is an ongoing endeavor. It requires discipline, persistence, and accountability. Leadership must be up to the task.

In 2013, a few years before I arrived at Salemtowne, the board identified the community as being in stage three (maturity stage) and moving toward stage four (declining stage) in the Organizational Life Cycle. Prior to 2013, in the mid-1990s and early 2000s, Salemtowne did an excellent job repositioning by adding new cottages, a new apartment complex, a new health care center, a fitness center, offices, and common spaces.

Before the great recession in 2008, the community had hit pause and managed the existing budget with little to no new growth for over ten years. In 2011–12, the board noticed that the census was dropping in the cottages and assisted living and the healthcare center needed replacing. The board engaged a consultant to lead them through a strategic planning process. Through this process, it became clear the time was right to work on repositioning. After the meetings, the board decided to reposition and engaged a consultant to lead the effort.

Once you've answered the question of timing, as Salemtowne did, the next question is: What kind of leadership do you need to reposition a community? The answer to this question starts with the board and moves on to the leadership team. A healthy board will recruit board leaders who can fulfill its mission and strategic plan. For example, at the time Salemtowne considered repositioning, the board had members with expertise in construction, architecture, and finance who understood the need to reposition and how to fund it.

On the leadership side, it helps to have leaders who have repositioning experience, whether that comes from the CEO, CFO, healthcare, or facilities departments. In addition, repositioning a community needs leaders who are skilled, future-minded communicators who are adaptable, team-oriented, and able to execute.

When its CEO decided to retire, Salemtowne was pressed to change leadership at the top. This led to an executive search that brought me into the picture.

Fortunately, I had experience with repositioning, and my background in development and construction provided a solid fit for Salemtowne's strategic focus — repositioning the campus by embarking on new construction, the first phase of which would be the new healthcare center. When I began my career as an administrator-in-training (AIT) at a Seattle community, I served as the owner's representative facilitating the construction of a skilled nursing facility (SNF), constructing a new third story of dual bedrooms, and remodeling all existing rooms on the bottom two floors with residents living in them. This seven-step process required moving residents from one phase to another so that the full remodel could be completed.

Another project that proved to be instrumental in preparing me for Salemtowne was working with a team to open a new CCRC in Silverdale, Washington, called Crista Shores. I also gained experience working for Covenant Living to raze an existing SNF and construct one of the organization's first neighborhood models of skilled nursing facilities—all private rooms with personal showers—and renovate an existing memory support center into a home-like setting.

Leveraging those experiences led me to ABHOW (American Baptist Homes of the West, now named HumanGood), where I became an executive director and a regional vice president managing five communities, each in different stages of repositioning and construction. Eventually, the organization sent me to China to start a joint venture and help leaders there develop communities in Beijing, Shanghai, and Guangzhou.

I had spent thirty years repositioning campuses across the country and around the world, and at Salemtowne I had the opportunity to do it again. Together, the board and I embarked on the journey to reach the repositioning goals.

2

LISTEN TO YOUR STAKEHOLDERS
IDENTIFY WHO IS MOST AFFECTED AND HEAR WHAT THEY HAVE TO SAY

"You just have to pay attention to what people need and what has not been done."
–Russel Simmons

Once you've determined the timing is right for repositioning, the next step is to discover whether the community's stakeholders are ready for the task ahead. What is a stakeholder? It is an individual or group that has a vested interest or is greatly impacted by a project's success or failure. To help determine who your stakeholders are and if they're ready for the journey, ask yourself these questions:

- Who will be impacted the most?
- What communication went out to residents and team members about the new project?
- Were all the stakeholders committed to moving ahead with repositioning or was there work to be done to unify the community?

Utilize Surveys

After accepting the position at Salemtowne, I wanted to know who the main stakeholders on the project were and if they were ready for the journey. To get this information, I started to assess Salemtowne stakeholders early — even before my first day on the job. I sent out customized stakeholder group surveys to board members, residents, the leadership team, and associates (employees) to learn what they liked about Salemtowne and what needed improvement (see Appendix A). I also set up separate Gmail accounts for the different stakeholder groups to come directly to me with confidentiality. Such surveys present an invaluable way to learn about the culture and how stakeholders regard the community. During my career I've learned that stakeholders, for the most part, will be honest and tell you what they think and feel.

I gathered some valuable information from the Salemtowne survey:

Residents: Most agreed on Salemtowne's friendliness. That trait is what attracted them to the community in the first place. They enjoyed their friends and loved living there. On the other hand, they believed communication could be improved. They felt the same about the landscaping and the long response to maintenance work orders.

Employees: The employees had a strong respect for residents and the core values of the organization and valued their co-worker relationships. However, employees identified two top weaknesses: poor communication and a lack of accountability among staff on all levels.

Leadership: The leadership esteemed what their colleagues brought to the team: experience and a strong reputation for quality healthcare.

Conversely, I could see that communication, teamwork, and administrative support needed improvement. The leadership survey also revealed a few power struggles going on. Not surprisingly, some silos existed.

Board: The board emphasized a caring and dedicated staff, excellent healthcare, and a strong commitment to the faith-based mission throughout the continuum of care as the organization's strengths. On the other hand, the board identified two areas that needed improvement: communication and the organization being too financially driven.

The survey also gave stakeholders a place to identify possible future opportunities. For example, residents encouraged more consistent pathways to communicate, employees and the leadership team saw opportunities to expand life enrichment programs and rehab partnerships, and the board envisioned the possibility of increasing memory support services, mentoring staff, and growing services for continuing care at home.

Assess through Focus Groups

After collating survey answers, I took time to meet with small groups of stakeholders to dig deeper into their written responses. I discovered in talking with residents that the new road leading to the new healthcare center had upset a large group of residents. Not only did the road cut into a number of backyards, it also disrupted a favorite park-like area residents enjoyed walking through.

In addition, I learned that the Salemtowne landscape crew had been downsized and replaced by a new landscape company a couple of weeks before I arrived. This had surprised residents, and they reported no prior communication about the decision. I discovered other issues that underscored the need to drastically improve communication. We had to get this right in order to cultivate stakeholder support for any new projects moving forward.

***

The results of the surveys and focus groups served as the foundation for crafting my 100-day plan, consisting of a written analysis and goals for the board. This plan also paved the way for some quick wins that would address the community's pain points (I found lots of help in Watkins's book *The First 90 Days: Proven Strategies for Getting Up to Speed Faster and Smarter*). I then kept the board apprised of my progress. Eventually, the goals morphed into the framework for adjusting the strategic plan, to be reviewed and updated on an annual basis.

Five months after starting at Salemtowne I sent out a New Year's letter to residents, team members, and board members. I shared what I had learned through the survey process and subsequent conversations and established a number of goals to address the areas needing improvement. Suggestions included:

- Implementing weekly construction meetings, monthly townhall meetings, and weekly "lunch and learns" with residents.

- Researching and implementing a resident-only portal connected to the internet.
- Initiating a monthly "Mark's Remarks" newsletter from the CEO to the residents summarizing what was going on that month.
- Evaluating core competencies of operations in marketing, information technology, healthcare services, activities, maintenance, housekeeping, security, and landscape services.

Once we put those strategies into place, communication improved. We initiated monthly town hall meetings to share announcements about upcoming activities and construction events, and I or other team members would answer any questions or concerns that had come up in the past month. This open forum helped build community. Prior to that time, town halls had been held quarterly.

The weekly construction meetings increased communication significantly. Most residents came to support the project, even as they understood that construction would cause disruptions. Blum Construction's site manager and our owner's representative led those meetings. They would share what had been accomplished over the previous week and the planned construction for the following week. This soon morphed into meetings held every two weeks. The meetings created a cadre of residents interested in learning about the construction process and tracking the next steps. The meetings also gave us the opportunity to share when roads would be blocked, or when ongoing resident life would be interrupted by the construction activity.

Finally, I made a point to have small group lunches with residents.

These occasions helped me learn names and the personal journeys of residents. As you can imagine, this went a long way toward building trust and demonstrating that I cared.

After the assessment process and quick wins from improved communication, we then updated the master site plan and strategic plan—another big undertaking, but now we had some wind in our sails.

3

LISTEN TO YOUR STAKEHOLDERS
CREATE YOUR COMMUNITY'S ROADMAP

"Change is the only constant in life. One's ability to adapt to those changes will determine your success in life."
–Benjamin Franklin

We all set goals, whether we do it on purpose or not. Have you ever been to Disneyland or Disney World? If you decided to attend either of the theme parks, you just set a goal. I grew up in Los Angeles, and I went to Disneyland more times than I can remember. In fact, we had E-tickets for the big rides. Back then, when you entered the gates to Disneyland, you paid for a book of tickets that had A, B, C, D, or E passes based on the size and popularity of the ride. Times have changed; now Disney theme parks have Fast Passes, a reservation system to get on rides faster by bypassing the long lines.

Sticking with the Disney analogy, once you decided to go, you made plans to travel and pay for lodging and figured out how to get on all your favorite rides before the park closed. Then you included your children and/or friends in negotiating an overall strategy so hopefully, everyone would be satisfied and happy with the results. By the end of the day, the outcome was often different than you had envisioned when you first started. What's more, how well everyone in your group was able to adapt to the unforeseen challenges of long lines and tired legs determined how many rides you were actually able to conquer (that was the real goal, wasn't it)? That is what I call a dynamic strategic plan!

When an organization starts the repositioning journey, leadership establishes the strategic master plan and begins to execute. But just like a trip to Disney, the plan frequently has to adjust to address unexpected challenges and new circumstances. The result envisioned at the start changes—which is okay. That's a sign of a dynamic plan and adaptive leaders.

The Strategic Plan: Your North Star

Adaptive leadership can make necessary pivots when the present environment changes. But having a strategic plan in place is important: It provides the structure that underpins adaptive change. The Covid-19 pandemic of 2020 was a great example of this, as many organizations, especially those caring for older adults, needed to drastically adjust to the constantly changing regulations to stay viable and open. Likewise, when you step into a new leadership role, unexpected challenges and new circumstances are guaranteed. The early days are like drinking from a fire hose. I call this "the whirlwind." The facility's strategic plan provides a relatively quick way to sort through the chaos, see what is most important, and determine where to focus energy and time. The strategic plan can become your North Star.

In all practicality, the strategic planning process allows the organization to define its future. When done well, the process also creates a collaboration between the organization's leadership team and the board, becoming a vehicle for setting goals and articulating strategies. A good plan takes into consideration the resources available and the many external factors the organization must deal with. Simply put, the plan lays out a roadmap.

Fortunately, I participated in several strategic planning processes early in my career. I used a couple of books to help guide this process: Bobb Biehl's *Masterplanning*[7] and Jim Horan's *The One Page Business Plan*[8] for Non-profit Organizations. From Biehl I learned how to use a planning arrow diagram to visually display the key elements of a strategic plan and how to effectively take boards through this planning process. From Jim Horan I discovered planning and monitoring systems, which aided my involvement in numerous annual strategic planning meetings. These experiences gave me the opportunity to work with Fresno Pacific University, Transformation Ministries, and several other organizations to facilitate their strategic plans. I used each of these opportunities to help grow my leadership skills.

Leadership, from the CEO to the board, needs to understand the existing strategic plan, identify key priorities, access any additional resources needed, and then update and implement the plan as circumstances change. The board needs to entrust the facilitation of future strategic planning to the CEO and the leadership team. The board can also use the strategic plan

---

[7] Bobb Biehl, *Masterplanning: A Complete Guide for Building a Strategic Plan for Your Business, Church, or Organization*, (B&H Publishing Group, 1997).

[8] Jim Horan, *The One Page Business Plan for Non-Profit Organizations: The Fastest, Easiest Way to Write a Business Plan*, (One Page Business Plan Co., 2006).

to monitor how the CEO is adapting to the organization. This tool can help bond the CEO and the board to make them an effective team to ensure the success of the organization. Repurposing a strategic plan involves a number of steps.

Understand the Existing Plan

The strategic planning process starts with understanding the existing plan and how it was developed.

Soon after arriving at Salemtowne, I researched the past minutes from the board of trustees meetings and came upon the approved strategic visioning initiatives of September 2013. These initiatives included five new initiatives:

- Create a master site plan.
- Create a holistic and comprehensive wellness program.
- Create business plans for nursing/rehab, assisted living, and memory Services.
- Enhance community areas throughout the campus.
- Implement new dining services option(s).

In addition, five other initiatives were already underway within the organization, and they needed attention as well:

- Execute updated marketing and pricing plans for filling and sustaining independent living units/apartments (ILUs).
- Launch Salemtowne's continuing care at home program, titled Navigation
- Upgrade technology infrastructure and systems.

- Improve dining technology, service, and quality levels.
- Board support for management's ongoing efforts to create a leadership development program and to formalize a succession planning process.

Doing this research was key to helping me understand the strategic plan and make future changes. For CEOs, leadership teams, and board members, clear communication of the strategic plan and allowing for questions and discussions is important to ensure everyone has a clear understanding of what's going on and where the organization is headed.

Identify Key Priorities

When I read the current and proposed strategic initiatives, I took a deep breath as I realized all the board expected of me. There were too many goals to accomplish in one year. After taking time to think this through, I knew I needed to identify priorities. How better to gather this information than to talk with the consultant who facilitated the board strategic planning process?

Fortunately, I knew Brian Schiff from my previous sixteen years at ABHOW. Back then, Schiff was a senior vice president of Greystone, and we worked together on a repositioning project in Fresno, California. Little did I know that he would become a close friend and would mentor me on a number of multifaceted aspects of repurposing life plan communities.

One of Schiff's practices was to set up a monthly project development team (PDT) meeting that he facilitated in person. The construction team (the architect, contractor, civil engineer, owner's representative, a couple of board members, and the leadership team) would get together and share their progress and next month's plans to keep the project moving forward and hopefully under budget. I attended this critical meeting to monitor our progress against our strategic plan so I could report to our bimonthly board meetings.

Access Outside Resources

After assuming my position as CEO in August 2015, I learned that the board had a tradition of holding a two-day retreat every January. I took advantage of this excellent opportunity to bring in an outside consultant to work with the board to update the strategic plan with some of our own goals and vision. I had recently learned that John Diffey had retired as CEO of Kendall, a multi-site life plan organization, and was available to facilitate our retreat along with Brian Schiff. (In 2021, John Diffey was inducted into the Continuing Care Hall of Fame in recognition of his forty-year impact on the field of senior living. Known as a champion of participative leadership and governance, diversity and inclusion, and outcomes in measurement practices, he was highly involved in LeadingAge as a member of the board of directors, a cofounding chair of the leadership development program, and president of the North Carolina chapter. In 2006, LeadingAge bestowed the Award of Honor on John to recognize his service and his unique ability to rally resources in the service of others in the aftermath of Hurricane Katrina.)

Even though I had experience leading other organizations in strategic planning, having an outside expert gave me the opportunity to participate in the discussions and share my observations and emerging vision. **Side note:** An outside expert may be perceived as having credibility to say things that a CEO might, with more impact--a good use of an outside voice.

The retreat produced Salemtowne's goals for 2016–2017, which focused on three areas:

1. Culture change, which would be addressed by implementing
    a. the Masterpiece Living Health and Fitness program to encourage residents and associates to adopt researched-based health habits of physical, mental, social and spiritual fitness; and
    b. Seniority's Ritz-Carlton Model Customer Service program, enhanced by a web-based learning program called Salemtowne Academy (Relias Learning [9]) to enrich our associates' learning and to develop a hospitality program.
2. Systems and operational structure improvement.
3. Implementation of one-page plans for each department.

In addition, the retreat produced board-originated goals for the CEO, consisting of the following:

1. Achieve good financial results (a board priority).
    a. Update existing systems to produce timely financial reports

---

[9] Abby Mayo, "Relias Named Top Ten of Top 100 Healthcare Tech Companies of 2023," *The Healthcare Technology Report,* October 30, 2023, https://www.relias.com.

including specified key performance indicators and a tracking/monitoring function.
  b. Align office staffing and resources thru DHG audit and benchmarking to support achieving financial goals.
2. Develop the leadership team.
  a. Complete new team structure and assignments.
3. Move forward with facilities and deferred maintenance.
  a. Complete capital plans, align staffing plan to benchmarks, review and update contracts.
4. Implement Navigation (Salemtowne's program for continuing care at home).
  a. Complete assessment, make decision on restructuring.
  b. Develop a business plan.
  c. Achieve approved goals of recruiting twenty-four new members per year.
5. Upgrade technology.
  a. Complete assessments, choose a new finance/healthcare management information system, schedule upgrades, set up employee training and adoption.
6. Carry out program development
  a. Establish policies, systems, and procedures for employee hiring, orientation, and annual training (Seniority Customer Service Program).
  b. Define focus and parameters and implement state-of-the-art program for resident aging health and wellness program

(Masterpiece Living).

c. Define and establish the highest quality possible memory support program (Best Friends program).

Implement the Updated Plan

Once the board set the direction, I worked with my leadership team to align their departmental goals with the board's strategic initiatives and my annual goals. We would always strive for collaboration. (See Appendix B for the Salemtowne operational goals by department).

The strategic plan for 2015–2016 (our fiscal year ran from April 1 to March 31) was reset five months after my arrival. We duplicated the process of updating the strategic plan every new fiscal year (voted in by the board).

The tradition of having a board retreat every January served Salemtowne well. The board chair and I discussed what the board needed in training. I would find the right consultant or professional to facilitate the retreat. Our board retreats focused on a variety of topics, for example, how to grow our single-site life plan community into a larger organization. Through those retreats, we learned from other CEOs how they had grown their communities into multiple sites. Consultants also educated us about new community developments, and finance experts like Ziegler explained to us the current financial trends and what we needed to do to obtain bond financing. Board experts presented a focused session about governance best practices, how to streamline our committees to focus on strategic/generative thinking, for example, and how to rethink our mission, vision, and values.

Strategic planning, a critical tool, helps the CEO, leadership team, and board keep their attention focused on guiding the organization into a successful and sustainable future. It truly is a North Star to follow during the journey of repositioning. And who knows, it may lead to a new Disneyland-type of life plan community.

PART TWO: REPOSITION FOR THE FUTURE
REPOSITIONING IS MORE THAN BRICKS AND MORTAR

"We shape our buildings; thereafter they shape us."
–Winston Churchill

An innovative pastor I worked for early in my career told me something I would never forget. "If you want to strategically help people," he said, "always think people, purpose, program, and property, in that order." In other words, people's needs drive purpose, which in turn drives programs to meet the people's needs. Property and buildings should support the programs that are designed to meet people's needs and that embody the purpose of the organization. When the people's needs change, programs must change, and property may need to change as well. I didn't know at the time that this pastor was describing a valuable set of principles that I would adopt for the rest of my career.

These principles hold true with repositioning life plan communities as well. The buildings get old and no longer meet the needs of those they serve. People's needs change over time in response to shifts in the economy, healthcare, wellness, technology, and other factors. New programs are needed to meet the new needs. And the physical structures must accommodate the new programs. For example, when I first started in this field, senior living communities rarely had fitness centers and weight rooms. Then research on successful aging proved that to stay healthier and mobile longer, weightlifting, aerobics, and stretching are crucial. Now it is almost unheard of to have a community without a fitness center.

***

Repositioning in marketing is the process a brand goes through to adjust its perception in the marketplace. The Cambridge dictionary defines repositioning as changing "the way people think of something, so that more people will like it, buy it, or support it."[10] The vice president of marketing says, "We want to reposition the brand in a way that says we're stylish and fun. This is about repositioning the company for the future." In senior living, repositioning includes marketing, but the task is so much bigger. The work is about changing the product and experience so that consumer perception changes. The work is about remodeling or replacing old buildings, erecting new buildings, creating new programs and products, and even changing cultures in order to stay competitive. Repositioning is more than building bricks and mortar, it is about meeting people's changing needs.

Constructing new buildings always includes the need to shift and adapt leadership, culture, and organizational structure. Why? Because new buildings, when intentionally designed, invite new ways of working, new behaviors, and new rituals, thus the need to reposition.

---

10 *Cambridge Dictionary*, "repositioning," accessed August 14, 2024, https://www.dictionary.cambridge.org/dictionary/english/repositioning.

4

REPOSITIONING LEADERSHIP
IT STARTS AND ENDS WITH LEADERSHIP

"Leadership is not about titles, positions, or flow charts. It is about one life influencing another."
–John C. Maxwell

Leadership is the keystone to enable any organization to reposition itself. In reality, leadership starts with the board of directors. The board shapes and blesses the strategic plan and monitors its progress. If the CEO is not executing the plan, the board may need to exercise its power to replace the CEO. But before it comes to that, the ideal arrangement is a partnership, with the board, the CEO, and the leadership team working hand in glove to implement the strategic plan.

As the executive director at The Terraces at San Joaquin Gardens in Fresno, California, my first day on the job was at the parent company's annual leadership meeting. There, all the executive directors and nursing home administrators of ten different life plan communities participated in a two-day retreat of training and celebration. They marked the Sydney Olympics with an Olympic-themed retreat. On the final evening, the company honored the achievements of most of the communities. They handed out bronze, silver, and gold medals for accomplishments over the past year. Wouldn't you know, nine communities received numerous medals. To my surprise, my new community received none!

I asked myself, "What do we need to do to change this?" Concerned about my community, I vowed this would never happen again. With a lot of hard work, leadership training and mentoring, in a few years the team achieved a top ranking among the company's best communities. The team also achieved many state and national awards and staff recognition. How did we do it? By working together, we transformed the leadership culture.

Transforming the Leadership Team

To begin the process of change at The Terraces, I first needed to assess what I had. I had learned that team members often have one of three types of responses to new initiatives and leadership change: balloons, floaters, or anchors.

Balloons embrace the new expectations with enthusiasm, engaging in discussions and working together to accomplish the goals.

Floaters adopt the new goals more slowly and work to keep the status quo. Not outwardly resistant to change, they have not yet embraced the new goals, thus "floating" between the new and the old.

Anchors tend to be the "nay-sayers" at every meeting. They resist the change and may even try to sabotage the vision by stopping any progress and "sinking" the initiative.

Your job as a leader in repositioning is to influence those around you, especially the ones in charge, to become balloons. Give them the resources and training to be successful, eliminate barriers, and allow them to soar. The way to do that is by first earning their respect.

Earn the Right to Lead

I love the saying, "People don't care how much you know until they know how much you care." John Maxwell understood that and wrote about it well in *The Five Levels of Leadership*.[11] Maxwell's five levels of leadership are:

- Level One: Position. The weakest level. People follow you because you have the job title, so they must follow you.
- Level Two: Permission (or Relationship). People follow you because they want to, as you have built a meaningful relationship.
- Level Three: Production (or Results). People follow you because of what you have done for the organization and the practical experience you bring to your role.
- Level Four: People Development (or Reproduction, which I call Mentoring). People follow you because of what you have done for them.
- Level Five: Pinnacle (or Respect). People follow you because of who you are and what you represent.

Following Maxwell's practice, on day one, I work at level two tasks to

---

11 John Maxwell, *The 5 Levels of Leadership: Proven Steps to Maximize Your Potential* (Center Street, 2011).

build relationships with my direct reports. This starts with survey questions about what they see as the best part of their job, their career journey, their family, hobbies, and interests (responses are all voluntary). For example, if they tell me about their children playing sports, it opens up space for a conversation about something other than work. I can ask on Friday, "Do you have any games this weekend?" And, if they do, I make sure on Monday to find out how the weekend went. It's a simple way to show I care about them as friends and colleagues working together.

Earning the right to lead can be challenging, especially with people who are more floaters than balloons. After the team sets goals, individual department supervisor goals come next. It is in individual meetings that I can gauge how employees are really doing. For floaters, after many years at the same job, many have developed comfortable routines. Uncomfortable with change, floaters may resist the new vision and goals established by the team.

Bruce Tuckman's stages of team development help to explain this phenomenon.[12] When a new leader or colleague enters an existing group, the group needs to re-form to a new dynamic, called the forming stage. As the group becomes more familiar with the new person(s), the group moves to the next stage: Storming. Tensions, chaos and frustration can arise as the group adapts and takes on a new dynamic. Tensions are normal, and communication is key to working through them. As the group adapts to

---

12 Bruce Tuckman, "Developmental Sequence in Small Groups," *Psychological Bulletin* 63, no. 4 (1965), 384–399.

new ways of doing things they enter a new normal. This stage, Norming, is the process of acceptance and leads to performing as a new group to the new standards and vision. Floaters will move through the norming process if they have opportunities to share and get to know team members better. I like using assessments such as Meyers-Briggs and StrengthsFinder and talking through results to understand each other's communication styles, strengths, motivations, and personality traits. Team-building experiences are another way to encourage working together. More frequent one-on-one meetings may also help to coach and encourage floaters to become balloons.

Unfortunately, not all team members desire to work together. In fact, occasionally you may come across an employee resisting or even sabotaging the organizational goals. These team members tend to bring other team members down and hence become organizational anchors. When working with anchors, I treat them the same way I treat others. However, after establishing goals and monitoring progress, in limited situations, I may need to bring in a coach or consultant to help critical leaders who are anchors commit to supporting the team goals and to establish healthy systems.

A personal coach has the ability as an outsider to observe resisting behaviors and share the negative impact the leader is causing to the team. The coach can share tools and ideas to enable the anchor to become dislodged and move toward a positive and constructive attitude. If outside resources fail to move the needle, then a formal personal improvement plan (PIP) can help. The last resort is to terminate the employee. In special political cases I may need a severance package to move the person on. Then it's essential to take the time to hire the right replacement and not rush just to fill a position.

Early in my career, I remember a director who tended to chronically complain and gossip. This person's attitude held the team back. This team leader was responsible for moving residents to the appropriate level of care. Unfortunately, they did not believe we needed assisted living services and kept residents in residential living way too long. We had a chronic census problem in assisted living because this person didn't do their job. This person was stuck in the old way of doing things and refused mentoring and engaging in the new culture. Eventually, after many failed attempts to help them succeed, they left after I reorganized and eliminated the position. The next day the leadership team felt extremely different, as if a rain cloud had been lifted. The problem of the assisted living census was soon corrected. Though things were not all roses, we continued the path to changing the culture of the leadership team. And I continued earning the right to lead.

Whether people are floaters or anchors, the point is to work on team building and improving relationships to convert those floaters and anchors into balloons that lift the energy and productivity of the team to higher levels.

Shifting the Culture

When I became CEO of Salemtowne, I implemented a system for shifting the leadership culture based on the above theories of team building. After evaluating all the stakeholder surveys, I observed the leadership culture tended to be siloed. Communication between departments was minimal, and the organization used antiquated technology systems. I set about changing the leadership culture through these steps:

1. **Become acquainted with department leaders through one-on-one meetings.**
   - Get to know leaders individually and review their survey responses in the meeting.
   - Understand their job by comparing their job description with how they explain what they do from the survey responses and in the personal interview.
   - See whether they manage their departments by key performance indicators (KPIs) or metrics. I like to call these vital signs, not unlike what a doctor measures—temperature, blood pressure and breathing—to understand if they are normal or are demonstrating illness and the need for treatment. KPIs (vital signs), must be monitored. I expect each department director to know their KPIs and check them daily, weekly, monthly, quarterly, and annually. When they see a negative fluctuation, I expect them to investigate the problem, discern the root cause, and correct the issue.
   - Understand the leaders' goals, accomplishments, and roadblocks.
   - Understand how each leader prefers to be supervised and how they would like me to communicate and manage them going forward.
   - Get to know each leader personally: what their passions and hobbies are, what motivates them, what their family situation

is, what attracted them to the organization, and what they like about working in the community. Again, people do not care how much you know until they know how much you care. New leaders earn the right to lead by showing interest in people as individuals, demonstrating competence, and communicating a clear, easy-to-accomplish, and follow vision.

2. **Share Your Leadership Values.** Leadership values (core beliefs and principles) help leaders manage others and achieve the organization's goals. Leadership values play a key role in how you make decisions and how you will respond to issues that arise. When working toward transforming the culture, you must first identify your own values and clearly communicate them to the team. It doesn't stop there. In turn, effective teams are also able to identify and clearly articulate their personal values. These shared values unite a team and give meaning and purpose to work. The next step is to agree on team values and to hold each other accountable to those agreed upon values.

I chose to develop the Leadership Values (LV) worksheet (Appendix C) to articulate my values and guide team members as they developed their own LVs. Once they completed their personal LVs, I had them share their values with the leadership team during the weekly meetings. Again, the key concept is to get the entire team to think about their leadership values, make the values explicit, and act on them. Then you can have each leader share their LVs with the team to help the team understand their peers' values and why they act the way they do. Finally, the leadership team can collaborate and develop team values stating how they will work together in the future. This practice can be life-changing for individuals and the team. LVs help unify the team and encourage accountability to live up to the stated values. Once established, leadership values can serve as a North Star, helping team members guide their direct reports.

3. **Add a thirty-minute leadership development time to the weekly team meeting.** This secret sauce strengthens a leadership team. The practice works because it brings team members' views on leadership to the surface, engages them in dialogue about leadership principles, and moves leaders toward application of the principles in each department. And the practice is easy to implement: Read a short essay or a book chapter, then ask the team members to offer their response, particularly their thoughts on whether the ideas would work in our community.

Helping a person grow in their career can be just as rewarding for you as a leader as it is for them professionally. I hired Jim Stacy as the director of facilities at The Terraces at San Joaquin Gardens. We met on a weekly basis, and he slowly took on more responsibility. After five years, the parent company promoted him to executive director at another community. Ultimately, he rose in senior management to become a regional vice president. Stacy now uses a similar learning model to mentor his leadership teams.

It's so rewarding to see people grow and take on greater leadership roles. I met Ann Cox, another example, when she served as the activity director at the Samarkand in Santa Barbara. She demonstrated great love for the residents and leadership potential. I saw how she not only accomplished her goals but solved problems and took the initiative to improve her program. A lifelong learner, she eagerly sought out new ideas on leadership and how she could apply those concepts. And she sought more responsibility. When the director of assisted living position opened up, I moved her into that position. Later, she became the nursing home administrator, a role she held for many years.

4. **Build a unified and synergetic team.** The hard work required to build a team needs consistency and perseverance. I would often start by reading and teaching Lencioni's book, *The Five Dysfunctions of a Team*. Lencioni believes that healthy teams trust each other: They freely share their ideas and recommendations to make team decisions, commit to decisions made, hold each other accountable to the team decisions, and focus on the achievement of collective results.[13]

Subsequently, by spending valuable time on leadership development every week, you can avert problems in the long

---

13 Patrick Lencioni, *The Five Dysfunctions of the Team* (Jossey-Bass, 2002), 188–190.

run and help others grow to their full potential. According to Muriel Call, "Leadership development is a catalyst that boosts employee morale, engagement and performance, supports professional and personal growth, and fosters a dynamic work environment. For employees, it's a valuable investment yielding improved retention, succession planning, collaboration and profitability."[14] What is not to like about that?

Lencioni's concepts make a solid platform to start from. I believe team members need to appreciate each other by knowing everyone's strengths, skills, traits, interests, and even hobbies, and to have common experiences together. You can employ different ways to accomplish this. Some leaders have monthly or quarterly team building events. Based upon the teams' interests and often geographical location, we have tried ropes courses, rock climbing, paintball, white water rafting, skeet shooting, axe throwing, museum tours, and miniature golf.

As mentioned, there is another way to build unified and synergetic teams: Utilize different behavioral assessments such as the Meyers-Briggs Type Indicator, StrengthsFinder, or DISC. These

---

14 Muriel Call, "Leadership Development: The Game-Changing Benefits for Employees and Employers," PeopleThriver, accessed August 8, 2024, https://peoplethriver.com/benefits-of-leadership-development/.

tools presented by a trained professional allow team members to reconnect with their strengths within the organization and gain a better appreciation for others and what they bring to the team.

Your goal is to create environments where team members can grow as leaders, build trust, become friends, and build supportive relationships as a team.

5. **Create Opportunities for Cross-Functional Team Projects.** From studies, we know that good working teams can boost morale, strengthen communication, and increase creativity, but transforming a culture also has practical, observable results when applied to team projects. I have discovered that getting the leadership team to complete a small project together changes the way they think. You can repeat this process with larger projects, building momentum and confidence that the team can succeed in completing most any project it sets out to do.

The Terraces at San Joaquin Gardens did this well. As a team, we envisioned how an old congregate care-assisted living building could find new life as a special care center for residents with memory loss. Once we converted the building, the corporate team saw our capability and put its full support behind us for a ten-year journey to renew our entire campus. We accomplished this complicated repositioning by including leaders from many departments to brainstorm ideas, devise a plan, and ride the wave of momentum.

In nine years at Salemtowne, our leadership team experienced the wave of momentum by working together on two major repositioning projects: The Babcock Healthcare Center and the Woodland Villas Independent Living Apartments. We also completed design drawings for a future third project. Shared success helps a team bond. And we knew we could handle complex new projects as we continued to grow together.

6. **Get the right people on the bus and the right people in the right seats.**[15] To borrow Jim Collins' teaching, I have found it very important to take the time and resources to hire a quality, experienced person. Exceptional leaders can raise the bar of excellence exponentially—not an easy task! Sometimes it takes more than a few tries to identify the right person for the job.

After the CFO left Salemtowne shortly after I arrived, I knew I needed to be patient in finding the right person to fill that role. After several years and two more CFOs, we found a CFO who fit and raised the financial bar for the community. Lincoln was a master at finding the right person and putting them in the right position. In Lincoln on Leadership,[16] Thomas explains Lincoln went through eight generals before he hired Grant to lead his army to success and end the Civil War. What I had learned from Lincoln, and my own more than thirty years of leadership experience,

---

15 Jim Collins, *Good to Great: Why Some Companies Make the Leap and Others Don't* (HarperCollins Publishers, 2001), 41.
16 Donald Thomas, *Lincoln on Leadership: Executive Strategies for Tough Times* (Warner Books, 1992).

was to persevere while building your leadership team. First, have a clear understanding of what each leadership position does, a clear picture of how they fit together as a team, and what is needed for the organization to succeed in accomplishing the strategic plan. In Lincoln's words, have a clear war policy and what is needed to win the war. Second, hire the individual you believe best fits your vision for the position. Next, give that leader the opportunity to succeed with coaching and observation.

Repositioning your leadership team builds a foundation for successfully repositioning your campus. The surprise along the way is to see your leadership team grow and become stronger leaders inside and outside of your organization. In the last nine years of my tenure at Salemtowne, we saw four of our leadership team accept CEO and executive director positions in other organizations. While we missed their contributions, Salemtowne is a better place for the time they spent there. Mentoring the next generation of leaders is well worth the investment!

5

REPOSITIONING CULTURE
SMALL CHANGES CAN MOVE MOUNTAINS

*"If you want to change the culture,
you will have to start changing the organization."*
–Mary Douglas

Part of repositioning for growth may call for a change in the community culture. When I started at Salemtowne, two of the strategic goals driven by the board of trustees were 1) to develop robust business plans to grow the skilled nursing, rehab, assisted living, and memory support services by creating industry-leading programs; and 2) to create a holistic and comprehensive residential wellness program with staged action plans. It's one thing to set goals, but quite another to create conditions in which goals can be achieved and sustained. These two strategic goals, critical to the trajectory of Salemtowne, required some significant culture change.

What Is Community Culture?

Every senior living community has a different culture. I experienced this as a regional vice president at two different communities in California.

The Fresno community reflected the city's rich agricultural history and was influenced by the surrounding San Joaquin Valley, considered a "breadbasket of the world." The Santa Barbara communities were shaped by a love of the arts, its small-town beach location, and a high cost of living. For instance, Santa Barbara has a median household income twelve percent greater than the median annual income across the entire state of California. Both communities had retired business professionals and leaders, and faculty and administrators from nearby universities and colleges. Yet each had a distinct character and differing expectations when it came to service.

Although location plays a significant role in shaping the community, culture is more than geographical distinctions and characteristics. Merriam-Webster offers specifics in its definition of culture:

a: The customary beliefs, social forms, and material traits of a racial, religious, or social group also: the characteristic features of everyday existence (such as diversions or a way of life) shared by people in a place or time.

b: the set of shared attitudes, values, goals, and practices that characterize an institution or organization.[17]

All of this is to say, that an organization's leaders can promote a positive, open, caring, and innovative culture through its shared values, programs, and practices. Or it can create a siloed, stagnant, competitive, critical culture looking for faults in people, which can nurture gossip and a

---

17 *Merriam-Webster Dictionary*, "culture," accessed May 8, 2024, https://www.merriam-webster.com/dictionary/culture.

hostile environment. Nonetheless, the ability of a community to shape its culture and thrive hinges on the organization's capacity to create intentional environments that foster growth and support openness to change. When it comes to repositioning, this often calls for a new mindset, re-examining existing attitudes and goals that characterize an organization.

Why Is Culture Change Important?

Cultural change is inevitable and often becomes necessary when addressing the numerous external shifts outside of the organization such as market demands, technological advances, changes in industry regulations, or societal expectations. It can also arise from internal organizational issues such as low morale or significant leadership change.

Life plan communities have experienced these challenges at exponential rates, and few can afford to take an organic or laissez-faire approach to change. Transforming a culture, particularly as it relates to repositioning for growth, is a complex process that calls for committed leadership, clear mission and vision, employee and resident engagement, a solid training program, and eventually, realignment of organizational structures, policies, and procedures to support the shift. Ultimately, culture change means creating an adaptive environment that supports the organizational mission, vision, and goals, encourages positive outcomes, and enables individuals at all levels to thrive. How is that done? As one of my earliest mentors would say, "It's about focusing first on people, purpose, program, and property—in that order!"

How Do You Reposition Culture?

Before starting at Salemtowne, I participated in several cultural change initiatives at ABHOW. First, I helped revise and implement a Ritz-Carlton customer service program. Second, I helped integrate a successful, companywide senior wellness and fitness program; and third, I helped develop and set up training of a special care memory support program called "The Best Friends Approach" by David Troxel and Virginia Bell.[18] Each of these programs were significant game-changers that proactively shaped the cultural fabric of the community. These three programs helped to answer the strategic goals set out by the board's strategic plan. But in order to improve the skilled nursing, rehab, assisted living, and memory support services, a robust customer service program needed to anchor the growth of the other programs.

Customer Service

For C-suite staff at a multi-site life plan community, each separate community has a unique customer service culture, usually based on the beliefs and values taught during the onboarding process for new hires, with behaviors reinforced by the existing employee culture.

This was the case in ABHOW communities. Early on, no signature customer service program existed that every community embraced, which resulted in hit-and-miss customer service at different locations. The need for

---

18 Virginia Bell and David Troxel, *The Best Friends Approach to Dementia Care, 2nd Edition* (Health Professions Press, 2017).

culture change was evident. Each community did its best to provide good customer service but experienced a variety of levels of satisfaction and areas of pain. Resident complaints demonstrated these pain points, which often ended up at the corporate home office. It became clear a system needed to be developed to guarantee consistent and excellent customer service for the residents and staff throughout all eleven communities in locations across the West Coast. ABHOW recognized this erratic culture and in 2008, the organization began an initiative to develop a signature customer service program. The mission to provide excellent care drove the initiative consistently at all its communities. The steps ABHOW took included:

1. **Identify your leaders and champions.** The former president of Seniority, ABHOW's subsidiary marketing, development and management firm, researched multiple customer service models. After many conversations and visits with well-known organizations, the Ritz-Carlton model was chosen.

    Why the Ritz-Carlton? In 1999 the hospitality company decided to share its best practices in developing a "world-class" quality organization by opening the Ritz-Carlton Leadership Center. This came after Ritz-Carlton won the coveted Malcom Baldrige Award for customer service.[19] In 2007, Training Magazine named the Ritz-Carlton Leadership Center the best global training company of the year. Ritz-Carlton also had the

---

19 Joseph Michelli, *The New Gold Standard: 5 Leadership Principles for Creating a Legendary Customer Experience Courtesy of the Ritz-Carlton Hotel Company"* (McGraw Hill, 2008), 9.

ability to train ABHOW staff and help the organization develop its own signature employee customer service program.

2. **Map out a plan.** Adopting new programs, especially those designed for deep culture change, do not occur overnight. Seniority spent a year consulting with the Ritz-Carlton Leadership Center to create a plan that became ABHOW's customized customer service program. And then Seniority branded the program as "Seniority Spirit," creating a campus-wide training process to help other senior living organizations fashion their own customer service programs.

After Seniority Spirit became a proven model, ABHOW decided to adopt the program for its life plan community division. We branded our world class customer service program as the "ABHOW Advantage."

3. **Train and integrate all stakeholders.** The ABHOW Advantage program took two years to develop and roll out to all eleven ABHOW life plan communities. To implement it, a steering committee was formed; I was a member of this committee charged with adapting the plan for ABHOW. The senior management team and the executive directors of the life plan communities spent a week of intense training at a Ritz-Carlton hotel. We experienced firsthand the world-famous customer service program while being trained in key principles, processes, and how to sustain the model. Many support resources were developed, including training manuals, employee recognition programs, and detailed PowerPoint slide decks with teaching notes embedded in each slide.

Systematically, we would train all employees in each department to the customer service principles. New employees sat in on a full day of training, and we set up recognition programs to reward team members whose service exceeded expectations. One of the most important tools was a daily training memo that emphasized individual customer service principles. A principle was shared in the daily huddle that every team member attended before each shift. This daily huddle was critical to sustain the customer service program. Residents also participated by documenting excellent customer service through the ABHOW Advantage recognition program.

I remember one exceptional example that occurred after the training was complete and the culture changed. When a resident lay in hospice dying, a cook wanted to demonstrate how much she cared for the resident. The cook took it upon herself to ask about the resident's favorite meal. That night, the cook went home to prepare this special meal and served it the next day. The delighted resident savored the meal. The following day, the resident passed away. What an act of love and sincere customer service by that cook!

4. **Evaluate and adjust.** No program is without its challenges. When the program initially rolled out, we immediately identified a problem. Clearly, not all the staff could be trained during their normal work hours. So, we brought a team of representatives together to evaluate the circumstances and devise an alternative

plan to accommodate shift schedules. This ended up being more costly but well worth the investment.

5. **Utilize outside resources.** To adapt ABHOW Advantage to Salemtowne, which we named "Salemtowne Shines" (Appendix D), I hired Teri Conklin from Seniority to help my leadership team roll out our culture change initiative. Conklin had significant experience helping other organizations adapt Seniority Spirit to their unique cultures. Another value I have picked up over the years: Using consultants to help implement initiatives I do not have the expertise to do. Sure, I did help roll out ABHOW Advantage, but I did not have experience adapting the program to another organization. I believed that this was a critical initiative to roll out, and I wanted to do it right and make sure the culture change was sustainable.

6. **Celebrate the outcome.** Lastly, we invited Salemtowne residents, family members, and team members to document employees going beyond their normal job descriptions to serve residents. On one rainy day, an individual observed a resident who had purchased groceries and needed to bring them into her apartment. One off-duty employee leaving the community saw the situation. The individual observed this employee rerouting his car to park next to the resident and help her cart her groceries in the rain to the apartment complex and up two floors to her room. This act of kindness reflects the values we so desire to exemplify and demonstrates that one action by one team member can make a difference.

Successful Aging

Early in my career, I was exposed to implementing successful aging programs at the communities I worked in. It all started in 1995 at the Samarkand in Santa Barbara. I worked with Nova Care, a rehabilitation firm that partnered with the Nautilus weightlifting company to create machines with lighter weights customized to help older adults maintain their muscle mass. The new research at the time discovered that after age forty, adults lost one pound of muscle mass a year unless they lifted weights. The studies showed that residents in skilled nursing could increase their muscle strength by 100 percent if they started lifting weights regularly.[20] (James Rippe, author of *Fit Over Forty,* was a heart surgeon and avid runner who researched why he was gaining weight even though he ran daily. He discovered that after the age of 40, adults lose muscle mass, which burns calories. The studies then showed that muscle mass does grow with regular weekly weightlifting, which helps to burn off the extra calories. The book is no longer in print. I remember it well because I developed a lecture series about the book to teach the concepts to residents who lived at the Samarkand.)

The rehab company (no longer in existence) developed a program for older adults with the Nautilus weightlifting machines called Vigor. At the Samarkand, we were privileged to be the first West Coast Life Plan Community to implement this program.

When I moved to San Joaquin Gardens with ABHOW, as one of my first cultural initiatives, we renovated a small, abandoned building close to

---

20   James Rippe, M.D., *Fit Over Forty* (Harper Perennial, 1997).

the dining room into a weightlifting gym modeled after the Vigor program. After teaching residents the benefits of weightlifting and exercising, we were able to raise funds for the remodel and buy the equipment. We hired a part-time physiatrist to run the gym for us. The program was well received by residents and team members. We were well on our way to changing the culture to include wellness.

In 2004 ABHOW convened a steering committee to review wellness programs for older adults and recommend one that ABHOW could shape into a signature program. This was of great interest to me, so—you guessed it!—I volunteered to be on the committee. We researched and interviewed eight national wellness programs. The most impressive program was Masterpiece Living. We liked the program because it was built on research about successful aging and incorporated a Mayo Clinic wellness assessment to tailor goals to each resident and monitor progress. Roger Landry tells the interesting story of the program's origin in his book *Live Long, Die Short*.[21] This book shares the breakthrough research on aging that approached the study from the perspective of answering the question of why some seniors aged better than others.

Roger and his brother Larry Landry, CFO of the MacArthur Foundation, decided to form Masterpiece Living to share the research concepts with older adults. A career Air Force flight surgeon for twenty-two years, Roger helped pilots and their crews stay healthy and perform

---

21 Roger Landry, *Live Long, Die Short: A Guide to Authentic Health and Successful Aging* (Greenleaf Group Book Press, 2014), 2.

their best. After Roger retired, he took on a second career to become president and CEO of Masterpiece Living.

Masterpiece Living's approach includes six steps:
1. Educate older adults on the research findings and what is possible.
2. Give them the opportunity to take the Mayo Clinic Lifestyle Inventory (an assessment of their current lifestyle).
3. Provide feedback.
4. Discuss the feedback in a one-on-one or group session with a lifestyle coordinator and set healthy living goals based on the research.
5. Foster empowerment with an authentic coaching relationship.
6. Repeat the Lifestyle Inventory and set goals every year.

ABHOW was one of the first multi-site life plan organizations to adopt Masterpiece Living as its signature program. All ABHOW life plan communities adopted and rolled out the program, and it made a major difference in the lives of ABHOW residents. Many residents implemented the wellness principles, which resulted in greater physical and mental health, fewer falls, the deepening of faith, the pursuit of personal passions, and service with others.

When I started as CEO at Salemtowne, I wanted to introduce Masterpiece Living right away. We followed the six steps of implementation and invited Roger Landry to be our keynote speaker at the kickoff celebration. It was an ideal initiative, as Salemtowne had already partnered with the Sticht Center for Healthy Aging at Wake Forest University School of

Medicine. This program was readily accepted by residents and gave us a common language and practical tools to encourage healthy living.

Memory Support

Our emphasis on customer service and successful aging at Salemtowne readied us for other culture changes in the new Babcock Healthcare Center, which opened in 2017. The new healthcare center shifted from an institutional design to a neighborhood design, which included one of the first Winston-Salem community rehabilitation centers, with two neighborhoods consisting of forty private rooms with private bathrooms and showers, and three long-term care neighborhoods with sixty similar private apartments. In addition, we created twenty private rooms for memory support and leveraged Bell and Troxel's "Best Friends" approach as our third culture-change initiative. We were fortunate to have Troxel personally train our healthcare team members multiple times and speak with residents and the greater Winston-Salem community about caring compassionately for family and friends with memory loss.

The Best Friends approach is a life-changing program that teaches all team members about the progression of dementia and trains the staff to treat each resident as a best friend. Early onset of dementia causes short-term memory skills to diminish first, long-term memory later. Through the Best Friends approach, team members are encouraged to learn as much about the resident as possible, including experiences, profession, hobbies, and family members, so they can converse and care as a "best friend."

Challenges of Adopting Programs

Culture change is difficult mainly because most people are comfortable with the status quo and change is an unknown. William Bridges' classic model[22] identifies three phases of a transition: 1) the ending (letting go), 2) the neutral zone, and 3) the new beginning.

In essence, this model applies to starting new programs. When commencing a new initiative, it begins with assessing those things you need to let go of; it is a time for endings and helping people deal with the losses. The neutral zone is the "in between" time where the old programs or property are no longer working and the new has not yet been implemented. This can be a time of confusion, doubt, and chaos, as well as a time of resistance and potential sabotage. The last phase is the new beginning, (where if we are honest, we would all like to start and not have to go through the pain of letting go). In this final phase, like a runner within sight of the finish line, there is renewed energy and revitalization, people develop a new identity, embrace the change, and make it the new normal in the community and the workplace.

Expect some chaos and unknowns. When we opened our new healthcare center at Salemtowne, we experienced the resistance and chaos Bridges talks about in his book. I have learned that when moving into new buildings, you can expect something to go wrong and some chaos. In 2017, the day we moved all residents from the old Phillips Healthcare Center into the new

---

22   William Bridges, *Managing Transitions: Making the Most of Change*, (Philadelphia: Da Capo Press, 2009), 4–5.

Babcock Healthcare Center, everything worked as planned. The resident council and team members greeted the skilled nursing residents at the front doors, escorted them to their new rooms, and helped them move in. There were many smiles, tears of joy, and much laughter. With the help of residents, staff, families, and board members, we accomplished our goal and moved all eighty-six residents in one day. Job completed!

The next day was when the problems started. You see, the old healthcare center was approximately the size of one football field. The new healthcare center was approximately the size of three football fields. Each neighborhood had twenty private rooms with private showers, a central outdoors courtyard, and a great room consisting of a living room, dining room, and an open kitchen at the entrance. We did not anticipate that when two CNAs were taking care of residents in their rooms behind the great room, the great room was vacant, and family members perceived there were no staff visible and available. The result was obvious: We received complaints from family members that we were understaffed. It took a while for our nursing staff to get used to the large spaces and to manage the team members to be visible while taking care of residents. We also needed to hire more team members, because the design was not conducive to sharing staff between neighborhoods.

The problems that arose gave us the opportunity to improve. We experienced firsthand that implementing programs in an effective and sustainable manner can significantly change the culture of a community. The Ritz-Carlton customer service program, the Masterpiece Living programs, and the Best Friends initiative, all game changers, transformed

Salemtowne culture in a positive way. In repositioning communities, people's needs drive the purpose for change and create the programs that buildings are designed for. But, before we get to repositioning buildings, sometimes boards of trustees need to be repositioned, as we experienced at Salemtowne.

6

REPOSITIONING THE BOARD OF DIRECTORS
YOUR BEST CHAMPION

"Without consultation, plans are frustrated, but with many counselors they succeed."
–Proverbs 15:22-23

A champion is a person who advocates for you and helps you be your best. Every CEO needs champions, and in business, that is the board of trustees. Research shows that a poorly managed bond between the CEO and the trustees of an organization can lead to a lack of trust and eventually undermine effective governance and performance.[23] On the contrary, a growing relationship between the CEO and the board brings synergy. As the relationship builds over time, the CEO can begin to evaluate how well the board adheres to best governance practices to ascertain how the board can become more effective.

---

23 Carolyn Dewar, Scott Keller and Vikram Malhotra, *CEO Excellence: The Six Mindsets that Distinguish the Best Leaders from the Rest* (Scribner, 2022).

My experience has taught me that healthy boards are open to a relationship of trust with the CEO, have a laser focus on strategic initiatives, embrace a learning environment, are mission-minded, and monitor the finances and progress of organizational goals. Most importantly, they are aware of evolving trends of the industry and have generative discussions about the direction of the organization.

Building Trust and Transparency

A healthy board relationship begins with trust. How does a CEO build trust and transparency with the board? As with the start of any relationship, it begins with getting to know the board members. When starting as a new CEO, I found it helpful to survey board members and read their responses before meeting with them individually. The surveys gave me insight into the members' personal stories as well as what they thought about the strengths and weaknesses of the community. Next, I met individually with each board member over a meal to get acquainted and ask questions prompted by reading their survey responses. I sincerely wanted to get to know them not only professionally but also as a friend by understanding their personal lives, goals, hobbies, family situations, the names of their children, etc.

You build trust by making promises and keeping them by doing what you said you would do. I made sure that I communicated with the board chair monthly, usually setting up a lunch to talk about community and board issues and goals. If I promised to accomplish a goal, I did my very best to complete it, and if I thought I might not succeed, I would talk to the chair, tell them why I might not succeed, and then renegotiate a new date.

A good conservative approach to building success and trust is to under-promise and over-deliver as another way.

You can also build trust by meeting with the executive council to share problems, share options, ask for advice, and set new goals to fix the problems. I remember during my start at Salemtowne, I concluded that I needed to remove a popular person on the leadership team. I carefully shared with the executive committee the reasons why I came to this conclusion and the plan I had to statistically validate my reasoning. Once I completed the audit that supported my decision, the committee agreed, and I executed a generous severance plan to terminate the person. This demonstrated transparency and laid the foundation for a trusting relationship moving forward.

Committing to Continuous Improvement

After establishing a trusting relationship, the CEO and the board can begin to identify opportunities to improve the board's effectiveness and efficiency. After working with the board for a few years at Salemtowne, I observed three areas that needed improvement: increasing the term of the chair from one year to two years, developing a consistent CEO annual performance evaluation, and reducing the number of standing committees.

Once these observations were shared with the board chair, we decided to use our annual board retreat to study best board governance practices to address how we could improve our board. This was the start of our repositioning the board for the future.

Changing Governance

Board members bring valuable skills and expertise to the organization. Adding governance training for board members will increase board relations and can have a significant return to the bottom line. At Salemtowne, we contacted Melissa Andrews, president of LeadingAge Virginia, also a certified nonprofit board consultant, to facilitate our annual board retreat to teach us board governance best practices. She acquainted us with the book *Governance as Leadership: Reframing the Work of Nonprofit Boards*.[24] The authors offer this "job description" for the board:

1. Set the organization's mission and overall strategy and modify both as needed.
2. Monitor organizational performance and hold management accountable.
3. Be fiscally responsible to ensure the finances are healthy and managed in an acceptable organized and legal manner. Ensure annual audits are completed.
4. Select, evaluate, support, and—if necessary—replace the CEO.
5. Develop and conserve the organization's resources—both funds and facilities.
6. Serve as a bridge and buffer between the organization and its environment; advocate for the organization and build support within the wider community.

---

24 Richard Chait, William Ryan and Barbara Taylor, *Governance as Leadership: Reframing the Work of Nonprofit Boards* (Wiley, 2005), 14.

The book also describes three types of governance:

Type I: Fiduciary or compliance thinking

Type II: Strategic Thinking

Type III: Generative Thinking

The goal of high-functioning boards is to operate as Type III, where goal-setting and direction-setting originate. When a board is generative, it has collaborative, creative, and paradigm-shifting discussions that move the organization into the future.

After the governance retreat, our board decided that we had too many standing committees: executive, finance, development (philanthropy), resident life, healthcare, and building and grounds. The last three committees had many residents on them, which encouraged the board to get more deeply involved in the day-to-day operations of the organization. These committees also encouraged the residents to go directly to board members with their problems instead of sharing grievances with management to resolve.

As a result of the retreat, the board updated the bylaws and reduced the number of committees from six to three—executive, finance/audit, and governance/nominating—and used one-off task groups when needed to address specific issues. We also changed the bylaws to reflect the board chair term from one to two years. Lastly, the board adopted a formal CEO performance evaluation. The retreat turned out to be an excellent collaborative effort to learn about high-functioning boards, to analyze our outdated practices, and to make changes to improve our effectiveness and strategic mindset. Here are a few questions to ask when you want to assess

the board's effectiveness and assess if it is time to reposition the board:
1. Is the board functioning according to its bylaws?
2. What bylaw changes have occurred over the past ten years, and why were the changes made?
3. Is the board high functioning, passive, or dysfunctional?
4. Is the board compliant, strategic, or generative in the way it functions?
5. Does the board clearly understand its role?
6. How many committees does the board have and what are their purposes?
7. Is the board diverse in membership?
8. What is the culture of the board and its tolerance for growth?
9. How does the board recruit new members?
10. How are board members chosen?
11. How is the CEO monitored? Does the board conduct an annual performance review?
12. Does the CEO have a succession policy and plan?
13. Does the board understand its role or is it heavily involved in operations?
14. Is the board well educated about life plan communities and current trends?
15. Is the board focused on achieving the strategic plan?

Experiencing Resistance

When the CEO and the board have built trust, created transparency, and worked collaboratively to improve, they can accomplish many goals to move the life plan community forward. But change may include some resistance. When boards plan to remodel or build new buildings, they will often experience some form of opposition. Good news--resistance is not all bad! It can cause an organization to step back, evaluate, and adjust if needed. Just like exercise, resistance can also make you stronger.

For example, a community in California was about to embark on a large-scale, $150,000,000 repositioning project. Because this was going to disrupt the community for over five years, multiple meetings occurred with residents and the resident council to discuss the plan, the length of time, and the rollout. Most residents were in favor of the project. They were aware they may be dislocated, but knew the results would significantly improve their lives and services. However, two couples did not want the project to move forward and continued to publicly voice their opinions.

After working with the corporate office, the board, and the resident council, we decided to offer each couple a full entrance fee refund even though their entrance fee amortization had expired. I talked with each couple individually, sharing that we did not want any residents to feel stuck in construction mode for many years and offered them a refund. To my shock, they both refused the offer. After many months and meetings, one couple was able to resolve their issues. The other couple did not resolve their feelings and moved out of the community, but understood it was their choice and did not expect the fee to be refunded. Through these months of challenging meetings, the real win was how the team worked together to solve the problem, and in the end became stronger for it.

On the contrary, sometimes resistance leads to other types of negative change and results. Another community was trying to obtain a multimillion-dollar bond to complete a repositioning project. The board had applied for bonds through the North Carolina Medical Care Commission and again, a few residents opposed the project. These few individuals started a letter campaign stating this project would cause the community to go bankrupt. They sent these letters to residents, city leaders, state leaders, and every state organization responsible for checking the financial validity of the project and approving the bonds. It even reached the state treasurer and governor's desk!

The board worked strategically to address these issues. However, the prolonged letter campaign resulted in the Department of Insurance pausing final approval of the loan for three months until all approving financial entities could gather for a town hall meeting with residents to explain why the project was financially sound and how it would help the community grow. Unfortunately, during the three-month waiting period, the bond interest rate increased by over 50 basis points, which cost the community approximately $4 million more in increased interest after the bond completed its term.

Moreover, even after the project's completion, letters continued from a few residents. Eventually the board created a "Persistent Resident Harassment Policy" and worked with the resident council to confront the individuals. Although you hope you never need to use such a policy, it does give the board and CEO leverage in managing an incident of significant magnitude.

Growing Board Experience

Working with boards is one aspect of being a leader of a senior living community. But as a CEO, you may also be expected to be a part of other boards outside your organization. People seek to serve on a board for many reasons, such as getting involved in the community, supporting a cause, or advancing their career. Early on in my career, a recruiter contacted me about a job in the Pacific Northwest. While preparing for the interview, I specifically remember the recruiter emphasizing the importance of having board experience. How does one acquire board experience? I asked my friend Steve Fleming, president/CEO of The Well-Spring Group in Greensboro, North Carolina, and 2017 Chair of the National LeadingAge Board and he said it well:

> "They say experience is the greatest teacher—I have found that serving on boards is a great experience for a CEO who reports to a board. How does one go about serving on a board? Start small and work your way up as they say... by small I think some of my first experiences were church related and Rotary. So that meant I had to join a church and get active and join a Rotary Club and get active...not to be so prescriptive nor to say one joins church for "business" reasons, faith should lead one to church, but the church is a nonprofit business too and it needs dedicated and engaged members to take volunteer committee and trustee roles. There are other civic clubs besides Rotary, but the point is to join one for the good they do, get involved, and as I suspect you'll eventually be asked to serve in a board/leadership role."

Fleming did just that. After serving on a few small nonprofit boards, he proceeded to the state trade association board—LeadingAge North Carolina—eventually serving as board chair from 2008–2010. He then worked with the state Nursing Home Administrator Board of Examiners, then the National LeadingAge board, ultimately serving as chair in 2017. Subsequently, Fleming noted that board experience can lead to another benefit, that of expanding your network. "Networking is an often overused word, but the truth is once folks know you are a willing, dedicated, and talented board member, word will get out."

I asked the same question to my friend Reed Vanderslik, president and CEO of Thrivemore in North Carolina, who had a different experience. His first board encounter was with a profitable furniture manufacturer. From this experience, he shared:

> "My first board experience was as the business development director with a territory in Asia and Latin America. I learned a lot about dealing with different cultures and practices in various countries. I also learned a lot about being sensitive to the fact that these board members don't know a lot about you and your business, and it is important to give background on the business and especially when making recommendations."

Vanderslik also worked on other boards, including affordable housing, some family-owned boards, and the YMCA. He shared that these boards gave him practice dealing with challenging situations, demonstrated the importance of board orientation, and showed that it is okay to expect board members to be financial supporters.

These two stories from seasoned professionals exhibit different journeys but the same process: Become educated about boards, step out and get involved, and be open to learning along the way. At the end of the day, board involvement is about building relationships and making a difference. A few other suggestions before getting involved:

1. Understand your motivation for getting involved and its importance to you.
2. Look for organizations that offer a good fit for your experience, skills, and talents.
3. Don't be afraid to volunteer first.
4. Know what is expected in terms of time and financial commitments.
5. Look to build lasting relationships with other board members.

The board that builds trust stays laser-focused on the mission and strategic initiatives, embraces change, is ready to address the challenges that transpire during the construction phase of repositioning, and can move a senior living community forward.

PART THREE: RENEW—MAKING IT HAPPEN
PLANNING IS MEANINGLESS UNLESS EXECUTED

> *"Good business leaders create a vision, articulate the vision, passionately own the vision, and relentlessly drive it to completion."*
> –Jack Welch

Teddy Roosevelt is considered one of the greatest presidents in U.S. history. One of his greatest achievements was to plan and start the building of the Panama Canal. The plan was to build a canal and a series of locks over fifty miles of mountainous territory to enable ships to pass though the isthmus of Panama from the Pacific Ocean to the Atlantic Ocean. The work began in 1903 and was completed 10 years later in 1914. The project included building one of the largest dams in the world and creating a large lake. The total project cost was more than $350 million, the largest cost of any U.S. project up to that time. A total of 56,000 people worked on the project and over 25,000 workers died by injury or disease.[25] President

---

25 History.com Editors, "Panama Canal," HISTORY, last updated August 13, 2024, originally published August 4, 2015, A&E Television Networks, accessed January 27, 2025, https://www.history.com/topics/landmarks/panama-canal.

Woodrow Wilson oversaw completion of the project.

The Panama Canal project had many moving complex parts. It took a team of international engineers, governments, treaties, and resources to complete. Repositioning communities is similar, at a much smaller scale. The important concept is that plans are useless unless they are backed by multiple teams, resources, and relentless commitment to see the project completed.

7

REPOSITIONING THE PHYSICAL—A PROCESS

REBUILDING MEANS CONSTANT RECONCEIVING

"Execution is the ability to mesh strategy with reality, align people with goals, and achieve the promised results."
–Lawrence Bossidy

As we discovered at Salemtowne, repositioning was a complex and challenging process that took many hands and a formalized, systematic approach to getting started. It involved a thorough analysis, a site plan and design, and of course, financing. As often happens, the Salemtowne experience included multiple phases and twists and turns on the road to repositioning.

Phase 1—Constructing the Babcock Healthcare Center

Construction on Salemtowne's Babcock Healthcare Center started my first month on the job, in August 2015. Brian Schiff, managing director of BS&A, and I would typically meet off-campus at Mid-Town Café for breakfast before the monthly project development team meeting to talk over the construction agenda, progress, and problems. He would order his usual sweet potato pancakes, and I always had a Denver omelet (salsa on the side) with pancakes. Of course, the most important ingredient was the pitcher of coffee. We drank lots of coffee at those meetings!

Early on I asked Brian why we started building a new healthcare center instead of new residential living apartments, which could generate revenue to pay for the new healthcare center. My experience was always to build apartments first. He said the board and administration believed new assisted living was needed first. Also, the market feasibility study concluded that the hospitals in Winston-Salem needed more rehabilitation beds, as Wake Forest Baptist Medical and Novant Health had to send rehabilitation patients to cities an hour or more away.

The feasibility study demonstrated that the new rehabilitation center paying Medicare A rates would help pay for the healthcare center. The former Phillips Healthcare Center could then be remodeled into a new assisted living building. The board wanted Salemtowne to be the healthcare center of choice in Winston-Salem to "leapfrog the market," in Schiff's words.

A lot of work had gone into making that strategic decision. The board hired BS&A to develop a new strategic plan in 2013. The consultants completed more than 100 interviews with residents, family, staff, and outside constituents, including agencies such as the Chamber of Commerce and the major hospital systems. They also reviewed Salemtowne's history regarding revenue drivers (i.e., pricing and occupancy) and operating expenses (i.e., staffing), as well as what the community had or hadn't spent on capital improvements. BS&A also completed a detailed market analysis to understand senior service opportunities in the Winston-Salem market.

The resulting strategic plan focused on:

1. The need to increase occupancy in residential living. This was a key driver for creating a better financial situation, as occupancy hovered between 80–85 percent.
2. The need and opportunity to reimagine the Phillips Healthcare Center. The community had redesigned the center fifteen years earlier with two beds to a room, but that now reflected a bygone era, as private rooms, private bathrooms with shower, and neighborhood design were the latest trends. Also, the plan called for the addition of a short-term rehabilitation program as well as new assisted living apartments. (No one liked the assisted living apartments in the fifty-year-old building!)
3. Expansion of residential living. The new apartments would be placed between the new healthcare center and the rest of the campus to create continuity and proximity to the amenities on the older side of the campus. Normally, residential apartments are more accretive and are built first to help offset the costs of healthcare buildings, which are not as accretive. The plan was primarily driven to first replace assisted living. A key factor: Salemtowne had received a donation of some fifty-six acres next door and had land to build on.

Brian explained (after more coffee!) that the consultants discovered the community was overstaffed in nearly every department. Aging buildings and poor operational practices often go hand in hand. The consultants recommended right sizing the staff.

The consultants also made recommendations to increase the census from the mid-eighties to the mid-nineties, to obtain bond financing. Monthly fees were lowered, and entrance fees were increased to balance out the mix.

Before this time, Salemtowne's policy was to neither expand nor allow interior walls to be adjusted in the community's cottages. This led to a census problem in the cottages. Once exterior and interior remodels were permitted, the census went up. A twenty percent discount for healthcare was also added to the contracts to entice census growth.

After Salemtowne implemented all the recommendations, it took about eighteen months to reach the 95 percent census needed for funding.

Following approval of the strategic plan, the community recruited a development team in 2014. RFPs were sent out to the various disciplines needed to plan a new project. CJMW was selected as the architect, Blum Construction as the contractor, Stimmel Associates for landscape and civil engineering, Jim Ruffin as the owner's representative, and Spectrum Marketing to help with sales and community pricing. Dickson Hughes Goodman did the financial feasibility study and Womble Bond Dickson was our legal counsel.

The design process continued through the summer of 2015 until the community obtained bond financing through Ziegler to build the new 120-bed healthcare center. So, a lot of activity was already in motion when

I arrived that August. The healthcare center plans called for a neighborhood design with twenty private rooms including private bathrooms plus showers, an outdoor courtyard, and a home environment with a living room, dining room, and serve-to-order kitchen. Six neighborhoods were envisioned: Two for short-term rehabilitation, three neighborhoods for long-term care, and one neighborhood for assisted-living memory support. Once the new healthcare center was built and full, the old Phillips building would be remodeled for assisted living.

The reasoning behind the timing of construction made sense. But I still saw a place where things could be done more efficiently. I asked if it would be possible to build residential living apartments at the same time as remodeling the old healthcare center. Brian agreed that new residential apartments would help strengthen Salemtowne's financial health. He then laid out the process of repositioning from the planning stage to the funding stage and, finally, to the building stage. Bond financing required a plan that captured all the critical components to repositioning.

A finance plan demands attention to several areas:

Analyzing market needs and financial feasibility requires market analysis for the project and creating a recommended scope.

The **design process** requires a master site plan and overall program design, conceptual/design drawings for the project, and construction drawings.

Financing the project requires defining project costs that include construction estimates and soft costs based on the conceptual design. You will need to generate a ten-year set of financial projections with project-associated revenue and expense items. To get permanent financing (for things like marketing, sales, and design activities), you must produce a plan both for the pre-finance capital needed and for the permanent financing of the project.

Implementing an action plan includes developing a marketing plan to execute the project, delineation of the risks associated with the plan and potential risk mitigation strategies, and a timeline and next steps for execution.

(The remainder of Brian's explanation expanded on the work plan, timeline and fees associated with providing such consulting services for Salemtowne. See Appendix E.)

***

Brian's detailed outline was new information for me. Even though I was in senior leadership at ABHOW, I was mostly involved with operations and design. The financing process was always handled by the CFO and the finance department. The entire process of repositioning is a heavy lift for a standalone life plan community like Salemtowne. I came away from our breakfast meetings with confidence in the process and the consultants Salemtowne hired to reposition the community.

Our next project was building two apartment buildings overlooking Salemtowne's wooded lake. I remember that the marketing and feasibility studies we completed demonstrated there were significant income-qualified senior adults within the primary market area that would make this project successful.

Phase 2—Constructing Woodland Villas

We began working with Alan Moore and Peter Epermanis from CJMW to design two hybrid apartment buildings called Woodland Villas. Hybrid apartments are designs that merge single-home dwellings designs with a smaller number of apartments on each floor. In this case, each building had on-grade parking under four stories with seven large, luxurious apartments per floor.

The goal was to design as many apartments as possible with large balconies overlooking the wooded lake. We spent many meetings reviewing different designs and angles to accomplish the goal. Pleased with the design, I affectionately nicknamed it the "batwing design," as it looked a bit like Batman's logo. We accomplished our goal: Five out of seven apartments on each floor had a view of the woods and lake.

We then went into pre-sale mode. We needed to collect $1,000 deposits for 75 percent of the fifty-six apartments to qualify for bond financing. The marketing study was correct: This was a desirable project, as it only took three months of advertising to collect the deposits. Unfortunately, we had to postpone construction for a year to fill up the rehab program at the new healthcare center. (Another reminder that the repositioning process often has unpredictable twists and turns that the organization must adapt to.) Once we filled up the rehab program, we were financially positioned to obtain bond financing for Woodland Villas. Our marketing team, led by Nikki Burris, did a fantastic job keeping our depositors engaged in building their community relationships while waiting for the construction to begin.

Construction went well—we completed the project on time and under budget. The only problem was, that we moved our first couple into the new Woodland Villas in March 2020, the same month that North Carolina shut down for what we at first thought would be a two-week quarantine due to the COVID-19 virus. That meant all new residents moving in during the quarantine months had to stay in their apartments for two weeks and could not visit common areas where they might spread COVID-19. The saving grace for the new residents was the large outside balconies, from which they could see and greet their neighbors. Some made it a practice in those quarantine days to enjoy happy hour together on their balconies or on the plaza.

The other great design feature was the outside plaza between the two Woodland Villas which had a fireplace, a fire pit, two built-in barbecues, and a water feature where residents would meet and get to know each other better. Resident gatherings were like university freshmen moving into their dorms in the first semester of school. These residents weathered the pandemic with fine spirits (no pun intended), and they became a well-connected and friendly group. We had allowed two years to fill the fifty-six apartments to 100 percent capacity, and it took only fourteen months in the middle of a pandemic!

Phase 3—Constructing the Next Repositioning Project

Once the Woodland Villas filled up, we started the next phase of repositioning to repurpose our older buildings with new hybrid buildings, a new assisted living building, a new kitchen with two new dining venues, and new physical fitness facilities. Repositioning continued as we welcomed more than 100 new residents to our campus, and we needed to build more common space for wellness and a new kitchen to replace the fifty-year-old kitchen. Also, we still had not solved the need for new assisted living apartments that could compete with those of newer communities in the area. The lesson here? Every ten to twenty years communities need to be repositioned, which means it should be an ongoing process. For Phase 3, we followed the same business plan outline laid out so well by Brian Schiff.

Craig Kimmel from RLPS, a Pennsylvania-based architectural firm, helped us update our master plan by leading a two-day charrette. The charrette experience gathered the leadership team, board members, and resident leaders to give observations and comments about potential new building designs. RLPS brought four different architects with their initial ideas about what Phase 3 could look like. Once opinions were discussed on the four potential concepts, the architects left the room to make adaptations to the designs. The charrette process continued one more time, resulting in the Phase 3 conceptual plan as well as multiple phases (4, 5, and 6) to replace the original fifty-year-old building with modern structures.

After many meetings of the planning development team, the board voted to start schematic and design drawings. Once the drawings were complete, we could start construction drawings, which would enable us to submit for bond financing. The marketing team did another great job collecting the $1,000 deposits in record time. Just before the board was ready to vote to move forward, the financial headwinds of 2023 hit. Construction costs escalated by one percent each month. Double-digit inflation rapidly increased, and the stock market fell 20 percent, dropping our numbers for "days cash on hand," a critical barometer for bond financing. Interest rates rose at an unprecedented rate as the Fed continued to try to bring down inflation. If that weren't enough, workforce wages went up from $9 to $15 dollars an hour.

Unfortunately, we had to hit the pause button on Phase 3 until we could raise our bond ratios to successfully obtain bond financing. Many other communities had to halt their construction plans, too. I have experienced these pauses a few times in my career at other organizations like ABHOW and Covenant Living. And I know there's a silver lining in these regrouping seasons: They prompt creativity, as designs and processes change to fit the economic downturns, often resulting in more efficient and better designs.

During this pause, we explored moving the existing assisted living residents into a remodeled area in the Babcock Healthcare Center, which would eliminate having to build a new assisted living building, saving millions of dollars. As an alternative, we looked at building new neighborhoods of cottages or mini hybrid apartment buildings (each mini hybrid would have between six to ten apartments to a small multistory building with on-grade parking underneath) where prospective residents' entrance fees could pay for the construction of the cottages/mini hybrids to increase our financing ratios. We hoped this plan would be cost-neutral, as entrance fees would pay for construction. However, after pricing out this model, we concluded it was too expensive to build. We also continued to grow our continuing care at home program, called Navigation, which would bring in new revenues. All these actions were designed to get back to funding Phase 3. Again, this real example demonstrates how repositioning projects need to be nimble and dynamic to adapt to changing financial circumstances.

The pause at Salemtowne was not the first I'd experienced. In the 1990s, ABHOW built a new life plan community in Silicon Valley during a recession. The organization had to pivot and reduce employees in all the Continuing Care Retirement Communities (CCRCs) to weather the economic downturn. It happened again during the Great Recession in 2008. ABHOW's life plan communities, like others, struggled to build up their low census as many prospective residents hesitated to sell their homes in the down market. Many life plan communities continue to pivot from the repercussions of the pandemic and the financial uncertainty of 2023. Regardless of the economic fluctuations, repositioning life plan communities on an ongoing basis is necessary to stay competitive in the market and current with the trends to serve seniors.

When to Reposition?

How do you know if repositioning will benefit your community? And what is the right time to do it? As you ponder, consider a few questions:

1. What is the goal, and does it match your mission?
2. Who is your target audience and who will most be affected?
3. How will this new service or program be different than what you are already doing?
4. What are your competitors doing, if anything, to meet the needs

in this area?

5. What resources do you have available to you?
6. What resources would you need to accomplish the goal?
7. How will you measure success?

As boards and leaders experience success in repositioning life plan communities, my involvement with LeadingAge both nationally and statewide proves very collaborative. I have appreciated the many mentors and peer support throughout my career, and the best way to end this book is to talk about mentoring and paying it forward.

8

THE LEGACY OF MENTORING
SUPPORT FROM ABOVE, BESIDE, AND BELOW

"The delicate balance of mentoring someone is not creating them in your own image but giving them the opportunity to create themselves."
–Steven Spielberg

I would be remiss to conclude a book on repositioning without mentioning the critical role of mentoring. One of the greatest advantages and most impactful roles of a leader is the ability to develop lifelong friendships and mentor others along the way. Do you remember when you first started your career? Chances are, someone believed in you, gave you your first job or simply bestowed wise advice on how to get ahead and accomplish your goals.

Derril Meyer, former CEO of Senior Services of CRISTA Ministries, was such a person for me. When I started exploring a career with nonprofit life plan communities, he would meet with me every two months. My goal: Become a CEO of a nonprofit life plan community in Seattle, Washington. After an initial meeting, Meyer told me that the quickest way to accomplish my goal involved first going through an administrator-in-training program to earn my nursing home administrator license. The next step: Get a job in the nonprofit retirement industry as soon as possible. I followed his advice and earned a license. Soon after, I became the nursing home administrator of the CRISTA Nursing Home. I am where I am today because Meyer chose to mentor me, and many like him, chose to mentor me and believed I "could."

Mentoring: What and Why?

We are all aware that mentoring is not new. Throughout the centuries, artisans have learned their trade from trusted mentors and apprentices. We see ancient examples of mentoring in Homer's Odessey, Jewish tradition, and Christian discipleship. More recently, we have seen a resurgence of the classical model of mentoring in numerous conferences, academic courses, and professional development venues. So, what is mentoring? Specifically, mentoring is a professional developmental relationship where an experienced individual (mentor) provides guidance, support, and advice to a less experienced individual (mentee). The mentor helps the mentee develop their career, enhance their professional performance, and achieve their goals. Mentoring can also include psychosocial support, where the mentor acts as a role model and support system.[26]

For CEOs and C-suite management in the retirement industry,

---

26 "Introduction to Mentoring: A Guide for Mentors and Mentees," American Psychological Association, accessed January 13, 2025, https://www.apa.org/education-career/grad/mentoring.

mentoring can be a powerful tool for succession planning, leadership development, and ensuring a smooth transition into a newly acquired position.

Practically speaking, mentoring is a trusted collaborative relationship that avails the leader of an additional thought partner, a tool to accelerate learning on the job or expanding your career options, and at the end of the day, a heads-up to potential opportunities, obstacles, and pitfalls.

A Model of Mentoring

So, why in this technologically advanced, social-media-heavy society are long-term mentoring relationships so hard to sustain? Or maybe a better question is: How can I integrate mentoring into my life in such a way that it becomes a lifelong practice? I believe the best way to do this is by embracing the idea of mentoring on multiple levels—the constellation model of mentoring:[27] Ask individuals who have accomplished what you want to accomplish to become your mentor, recruit peers to bounce ideas off of, ask for guidance, and find those who need mentoring from you. That is the constellation model—incorporating a *generational mentality* of being mentored from above you, next to you, and mentoring others below you (those who have less experience than you in your industry), all at once. Integrating experienced mentors, current peer colleagues, and up-

---

[27] Maureen Vandermaas-Peeler, "Mentoring for Learner Success: Conceptualizing Constellations," Elon University Center for Engaged Learning (blog), accessed February 18, 2021, https://www.centerforengagedlearning.org/mentoring-for-learner-success-conceptualizing-constellations.

and-coming professionals into your network constitutes a constellation of resources and wisdom that can go beyond finding the next best job and can help you build your very own support team that can follow you throughout your career and life journey.

How to Build Your Personal Network and Support Team of Mentors

Building a strong personal network and assembling a team of mentors is pivotal for professionals in the nonprofit senior services sector. The benefits of having a well-rounded network and trusted mentors can't be overstated. They provide guidance, support, and valuable industry insights that help you grow both personally and professionally. Here are a few steps to help you build your support team of mentors:

Identify your goals and needs. Before you start networking, it's essential to understand your personal and professional goals. Are you looking to advance your career, gain specific skills, or expand your knowledge base? Knowing what you want will help you identify the right people to connect with. Consider performing a self-assessment to pinpoint your strengths, weaknesses, opportunities, and threats (to do a SWOT analysis). This clarity will direct your networking efforts toward individuals who can best support your journey.

Engage in industry events. Attend industry events, such as conferences, workshops, and seminars. These gatherings are prime opportunities to meet like-minded professionals. Engage actively in discussions and don't hesitate to introduce yourself to speakers and fellow attendees.

Before attending these events, prepare by researching the speakers and attendees, so you can have meaningful conversations and ask insightful questions. Bring business cards and follow up with new contacts to keep the connection alive.

Utilize online platforms. Leverage online platforms like LinkedIn to connect with industry professionals. Join relevant groups and participate in discussions. Share your experiences and insights to establish yourself as a thought leader in the senior services sector. Regularly update your profile to reflect your achievements and interests and engage with content posted by others to increase your visibility. Participating in webinars and online forums can also help you stay informed about the latest trends and build connections across geographical boundaries.

Seek out diverse perspectives. Don't limit your network to those within your immediate field. Engage with professionals from related industries to gain a broader perspective. This diversity can provide unique insights and innovative solutions to common challenges. For example, connecting with professionals in healthcare, technology, and community services can give you new ideas on improving senior care services. Attend interdisciplinary events and join cross-industry groups to broaden your horizons.

Nurture Your Relationships. Building a network isn't just about making connections—it's about maintaining them. Follow up with new contacts, set up regular check-ins, and offer support when you can. Building trust and mutual respect is key to a strong network.

Consider scheduling periodic catch-up meetings or coffee chats to keep the relationship warm. Don't hesitate to share relevant resources, articles, or opportunities with your connections to add value to your relationship.

Identify potential mentors. Look for experienced professionals who have a track record of success in your field. Approach them with a clear idea of what you hope to gain from the mentoring relationship and what you can offer in return. Be specific about the areas where you need guidance and how their experience aligns with your career goals. Be respectful of their time and show genuine interest in their insights and advice.

Embrace the constellation model. Constellation mentoring is having a diverse group of mentors and mentees: those who have gone before you, those who walk alongside you, and those you can mentor. Mentors guide, challenge, advocate for, and champion your career. Much like stars in a constellation, these mentors provide different perspectives and expertise, creating a comprehensive support system that helps you navigate your career path. This approach allows you to benefit from a range of experiences and knowledge, ensuring you receive well-rounded advice and support as well as the opportunity to guide others.

Be proactive and open to learning. Mentoring is a two-way street. Be open to feedback and willing to learn. Show your mentors that you value their time and insights by taking their advice seriously and acting on it. Keep them informed about your progress and achievements, and express gratitude for their guidance. Demonstrating your commitment to personal and professional growth will encourage mentors to invest in your development further.

By actively building your network and support team, you'll not only enhance your career but also contribute to the growth and improvement of the nonprofit senior services field. A strong network and mentoring team can help you stay informed about industry trends, overcome challenges, and find new opportunities to make a meaningful impact.

Stories of Stellar Mentors

One exemplary mentor who helped me was Kay Kallander, who hired me for my first executive director job at San Joaquin Gardens in Fresno, California. Kay, at the time, was the COO at ABHOW. She mentored me for sixteen years, supporting me in the organization and advocating for me as I moved into a regional role and then a presidential role in China.

Beyond my personal experience with Kallander, she became a national mentor when Larry Minnix, the president of LeadingAge in 2007, challenged the association to develop a leadership academy to help produce new leaders for our association. Larry first asked Michelle Holleran and Judy Brown to develop the program and curriculum before the next LeadingAge annual meeting. During the development of the program, Michelle called upon Kallander and John Diffey to become the professional coaches to the first starting class of thirty mentees.

Kallander continued in the national coaching role for several years until she decided to develop a similar program for ABHOW to advance emerging leaders within the organization to ensure a succession line of future leaders. Kallander asked Holleran to help her implement the ABHOW leadership academy, named Leadership ABHOW. Kallander did not stop there. She then became very involved in LeadingAge California and again asked Holleran to help start a LeadingAge of California leadership academy named Emerge. Holleran went on to help open twelve LeadingAge state leadership academies and continues to consult and coach.

No matter what stage you are in your career, you can benefit from mentoring. Kallander continues to mentor today. After Kallander retired, Katie Smith Sloan, the president of LeadingAge, asked her to start an international academy. She took the program to France and Australia during the early years of The Global Ageing Network annual meetings. After I interviewed Kallander, she told me that she had recently worked with her local Chamber of Commerce in Redlands, California, to start their Leadership Redlands mentoring program. Kallendar's passion for facilitating the progress of others has inspired numerous leaders in the field to be lifelong learners and mentors.

Another form of mentoring is for colleagues and peers with similar experiences to gather on a regular basis to share and discuss current issues and concerns. For me, this was the CEO Roundtable, a small North Carolina group of local retirement community CEOs. During the Covid-19 pandemic, Andrew Applegate, CEO of nearby Arbor Acres, and I would meet weekly via Zoom to compare how we were adapting to the new Covid rules from the Center for Medicare and Medicaid Services (CMS), which changed almost weekly. We then invited other peers in our region to participate: Reid Vanderslik, CEO of Thrivemore; Steve Fleming, CEO of Wellspring; and Tim Webster, CEO of Brightspire. We found it a great help to ponder the changes and exchange ideas on how to keep our residents and team members safe during the crisis. After things began to stabilize, we changed the format to meeting monthly at a brewery and named our group the CEO Roundtable. This fellowship served as a great resource for answering questions regarding program ideas, policies, and how different situations have been handled in one another's communities. It became a kind of a life plan community CEO think tank and has built meaningful friendships.

My last example of a model mentor is Karl Yena, one of many of the inspiring residents at Salemtowne, who worked for Reynolds Tobacco for thirty-three years, retiring from RJR Nabisco in 1998 as a senior level manager. He provided consulting services to RJR corporations and fourteen acquired companies, both domestic and international. These included Nabisco, Kentucky Fried Chicken, Del Monte, Sea Land Shipping, and many others. In addition, he assessed newly acquired companies for efficiency, analyzed the organizational structure, and developed efficiency plans that he monitored, coached, and consulted through the integration stage, usually for over a year. He developed training programs with professors from MIT, Harvard, Stanford, and Columbia for these companies, both domestically and internationally.

After retiring, Yena felt he still had much to contribute, so he continued to coach and consult over a for the next twenty-eight years. During his last eight years, he continued to mentor CEOs and organizations at no charge. He is a volunteer consultant for over 100 nonprofits and for-profit firms annually and typically coaches/mentors at least ten CEOs consistently throughout the year.

What makes Yena so inspiring is that he has lots of energy and a positive outlook on life, learns constantly, and is excited about helping leaders and organizations whenever he can. He has made a significant difference in Winston-Salem these past twenty-eight years and has received numerous volunteer awards.

Like these exemplary lifetime leaders and mentors, I want to challenge you to commit to lifelong mentoring in your current career into your retirement and beyond to continue making a difference in the constellation of lives you touch every day.

AFTERWORD

As I write this, Salemtowne's repositioning is not complete, which I feel is a fitting conclusion for this book. Repositioning becomes an ongoing process for a life plan community. We're always learning and applying lessons to the next project.

The lessons learned are many, for renewal involves much more than just bricks and mortar. I believe it starts in the soul, a passion to serve older adults in the fourth quarter of their lives. It involves a commitment to developing quality programs and buildings to improve older adults' lives and to help them live healthier and longer so that they can continue to pursue their passions and dreams.

I remember when we built our new neighborhood healthcare center at The Terraces at San Joaquin Gardens and moved our skilled nursing residents from the old to the new. One of our residents wept tears of joy. She said, "I never believed I could spend my last days in such a beautiful place."

I wish that dear woman could have been my mom. I had asked Mom if she wanted to move closer to us, and she refused, saying it would be too difficult at this time in her life to start anew.

I have been blessed by this great mission-driven, nonprofit field to serve older adults. My passion for repositioning life plan communities was cultivated over the years by serving alongside many great leaders. This rewarding career has provided many opportunities to improve services and develop new programs and new buildings with a purpose that improves the lives of older adults.

Repositioning is complicated and takes many twists and turns. It involves understanding where your organization is in the lifecycle, assessing your stakeholders, digging deep into the strategic plan, growing your leadership team, making culture changes, building an effective board relationship, and, finally, realizing that those who have come before, stand beside us, and come after us are all vital to the work of renewal.

I hope that as you progress on your journey, you too will find inspiration for improving the lives of others through repositioning.

ACKNOWLEDGMENTS

I want to thank the many people who have supported me throughout my career in leading life plan communities and inspired me to write this book.

First, thanks to God and my faith in Jesus Christ who gives me the passion to make a positive difference in people's lives and who guided me throughout my life through the good times and the difficult times.

Second, thanks to my wife, Cindy, who encouraged me, discussed ideas, and edited early drafts. I love and respect my wife dearly, and I cannot imagine living my life without her. Thanks to my grown children and their families who supported me and whom I love very much.

Third, thanks to my friend Daniel Pryfogle, who encouraged me to write this book and who edited and guided me through the publishing process. As well as thanks to Karen Alley and Rita Lewis for editing my manuscript.

I thank my father, Garth, who taught me character, faith, leadership, and innovation; my mother, Marjorie, who taught me compassion and how to age successfully and gracefully; and my brother, Dave, who had a successful career in the senior living field and encouraged, supported, and guided me through the leadership journey.

I'd also like to thank those who guided and mentored me in the career journey: Larry Dewitt of Calvary Community Church, who taught me how to manage and lead; Mike Martin of Christa Ministries, who gave me my first job as a nursing home administrator and the opportunity to help open a new life plan community in Silverdale, Washington; Steve Anderson of Covenant Living, who was my best boss; Kay Kallander of ABHOW, who believed in me and hired me as an executive director to manage my first life plan community; Dave Ferguson of ABHOW, who challenged me to the limits of my potential to consult and start a business in China; Joe Anderson of ABHOW, who worked with me in China and saw the significant opportunity to help improve China's aging programs; David Troxel, who taught me how to passionately care for those with dementia and memory loss; Roger Landry, who drew upon research to teach me how to successfully age and to teach others these principles; Tom Akins of LeadingAge North Carolina, who mentored me and oriented me to the politics of North Carolina; and Melissa Andrews of LeadingAge Virginia, who guided me through board repositioning.

The project development team who taught me the details of repositioning and funding projects was extremely helpful to me. They included Brian Schiff and Tonya Bodie with BS&A, who facilitated the team; Tommy Brewer with Ziegler; David Broughton with Womble Bond Dickinson, Alan Moore; Peter Epermanis with CJMW; Craig Kimmel with RLPS; Drew Hancock; Mark Dunigan with Blum Construction; Neal Tucker with Stimmel; Jim Ruffin and Stewart Beason, owner's representatives; Melissa Pritchard with SFCS; Keith Seeloff with Forvis; and Rob Love, of Love and Company.

ACKNOWLEDGMENTS

Last but not least, I'd like to thank those who supported me through the repositioning journey at Salemtowne. These included the board chairs who had the vision to reposition, and who hired and supported me to execute that vision: Frank James, Peggy Carter, Darin Mabe, Kim Stogner, Chris Perry, John Geis, and Marty Edwards. The resident council chairs who worked with me to encourage collaboration between residents and Salemtowne leadership were extremely helpful: Joyce Swayne, Sue Hendricks, Harry Harkey, Joan Lide, and Dave Jones. Ginny Simpson who helped with editing. And, finally, I'd like to thank the incredible leadership team who made repositioning happen: Tracy Biesecker, Nikki Burris, Allison Vessels, Emily Rector, Tim Dahlke, Eric Kirkeeng, and Cecania Branch.

APPENDIX A
SURVEYS

Surveys are an important tool used to review and assess the key stakeholders in a life plan community. I sent the following surveys one month before I started my job in Salemtowne. This gave me the opportunity to compile and contrast the observations and perceptions of stakeholders about Salemtowne. The following questions are similar and can be customized toward each specific stakeholder group.

Board Member Survey

1. Please tell me about yourself (your name, family, job, hobbies, how long you have lived in the area, etc.)
2. Why did you choose to become a board member at Salemtowne?
3. What is the heart and mission of Salemtowne in your own words?
4. What works well at Salemtowne?
5. What can be improved at Salemtowne?
6. Please rank the top CCRCs in the Triad from 1–5. Why did you rank Salemtowne as you did?
7. If you had a magic wand and would change anything in Salemtowne

today, what would it be?
8. What would you never change at Salemtowne?
9. What do you like about living in the Winston-Salem area?
10. What advice do you have for me to start well at Salemtowne?
    a. What do you hope I will do?
    b. What are you concerned about what I might do?
    c. What are you concerned I might not do?
    d. Anything else I should know or ask before I arrive?

Resident Survey

1. Please tell me about yourself (your name, family, job, hobbies, how long you have lived in Salemtowne, etc.)
2. Why did you choose to live in Salemtowne?
3. What is the heart and mission of Salemtowne in your own words?
4. What do you like about living here?
5. What can be improved?
6. Please rank the top CCRCs in the Triad from 1–5. Why did you rank Salemtowne as you did?
7. If you had a magic wand and would change anything in Salemtowne today, what would it be?
8. What would you never change at Salemtowne?
9. What do you like about living in the Winston-Salem area?
10. What advice do you have for me to start well at Salemtowne?
    a. What do you hope I will do?
    b. What are you concerned about what I might do?

c. What are you concerned I might not do?

   d. Anything else I should know or ask before I arrive?

Leadership Survey

1. Please tell me about yourself (your name, family, job, hobbies, how long you have worked at Salemtowne, etc.)
2. Why did you choose to work at Salemtowne?
3. What is the heart and mission of Salemtowne in your own words?
4. What do you like about working here?
5. What can be improved?
6. What do you like about living in the Winston-Salem area?
7. Please rank the top CCRCs in the Triad from 1–5. Why did you rank Salemtowne as you did?
8. If you had a magic wand and would change anything in Salemtowne today, what would it be?
9. What would you never change at Salemtowne?
10. What is your leadership philosophy?
11. What are your goals for your area of responsibility for 2015 and what is your progress towards accomplishing them?
12. What are your values about teamwork? What has been your experience on how you would build teamwork?
13. What are the vital signs of your area of responsibility? In other words, what Key Performance Indicators or metrics do you use to know the health of your area of responsibility?

    a. Key performance indicators

     b. What is the health of your area of responsibility?

     c. What works well in your area of responsibility?

     d. What would you like to improve in your area of responsibility?

14. Please write a SWOT analysis of your area of responsibility.

     a. Strengths

     b. Weaknesses

     c. Opportunities

     d. Threats

15. Please write a SWOT analysis of the Salemtowne operations.

     a. Strengths

     b. Weaknesses

     c. Opportunities

     d. Threats

16. What advice do you have for me to start well at Salemtowne?

     a. What do you hope I will do?

     b. What are you concerned about what I might do?

     c. What are you concerned I might not do?

     d. Anything else I should know or ask before I arrive?

Team Member Survey

1. Please tell me about yourself.
2. Why did you choose to work at Salemtowne?
3. What is the heart and mission of Salemtowne in your own words?
4. What do you like about working here?
5. What can be improved?

APPENDIX A

6. What do you like about living in the Winston Salem area?
7. Please rank the top CCRCs in the Triad from 1-5. Why did you rank Salemtowne as you did?
8. If you had a magic wand and would change anything in Salemtowne today, what would it be?
9. What would you never change at Salemtowne?
10. What advice do you have for me to start well at Salemtowne?
    a. What do you hope I will do?
    b. What are you concerned I might not do?
    c. Anything else I should know or ask before I arrive?

APPENDIX B

SALEMTOWNE OPERATIONAL GOALS BY DEPARTMENT

Life Enrichment

1. Achieve Budget by 3/31/17
2. Implement Masterpiece Living by 12/1/16
3. Continue to develop the Sticht Center partnership and complete the Assessment App by 3/31/17
4. Implement Best Friends program for memory support with Jay by 3/31/17
5. Assess and develop Healthy Fitness plans for 40% of IL residents by 3/31/17
6. To create and implement a Grief support program for residents by 7/1/16
7. Negotiate WFBH CareNet collaboration by 1/1/17

Marketing and Sales

1. Achieve Budget by 3/31/17
2. Sustain 95% occupancy in IL by 3/31/17
3. Collect 37 10% sales deposits for Phase III by 3/31/17

4. Complete new floor plan options (and remodel standards) for cottages and apartments by 10/1/16
5. Implement and manage Salemtowne and Navigation Marketing and Advertisement program with Love and Co. by 9/1/16.

Finance

1. Achieve Budget by 3/31/17
2. Upgrade Finance systems to result in efficient, timely reports (with KPI), accounts payable and billing by 11/1/16
3. Implement electronic document storage system by 3/31/17
4. Expand receptionist coverage to cover weekends and to be trained as concierges by 9/1/16
5. Develop and implement a PTO tracking system to ensure PTO is taken in a timely manner by 10/1/16

Health Care

1. Achieve Budget by 3/31/17
2. Obtain Home Care license and/or waiver by 1/1/17
3. Achieve superior survey (metric TBD) in 2016 (Goal: to achieve 5 star rating)
4. Implement levels of care fee structure to improve quality of care in AL by 12/1/16
5. Implement Best Friends program in memory support with Liz by 3/31/17
6. Develop an opening plan to transition HCC to new building in

2017 by 3/31/17

Dining

1. Achieve Budget by 3/31/17
2. Open one new dinning venue by 1/1/17
3. Remodel Babcock Kitchen for dining events and a potential 3rd dinning venue by 7/1/16
4. Implement quarterly Upscale dinner for residents with courses and wine pairings by 6/1/16
5. Obtain average 85% resident satisfaction surveys from residents regarding dining experience by 3/31/17

Facilities

1. Achieve Budget by 3/31/17
2. Complete agreed upon capital projects by 3/31/2017
3. Implement Sodexo management contract by 10/1/16
4. Organize Facilities offices and storage by 7/1/16
5. Complete gating campus and mobilizing night security guard by 9/1/16

Navigation

1. Achieve Budget by 3/31/17
2. Sign up 20 new contracts totaling 37 (including attrition) by 3/31/17
3. Develop and implement marketing and tactical business plans by

7/1/16
4. Create and implement new bridge product allowing Navigation residents to move into Salemtowne by 8/1/16
5. Implement a once a month social events program by 3/31/17

Development

1. Achieve Budget by 3/31/17
2. Achieve Pathway Campaign goal of $2 M by 3/31/17
3. Develop and implement estate planning educational and event program once a quarter by 7/1/17
4. Research and implement planned giving software 2/1/17
5. Develop and implement annual associate ST campaign by 3/31/17

Human Resources

1. Achieve Budget by 3/31/17
2. Implement Salemtowne Academy by 7/1/16
3. Implement Seniority Customer Service program by 3/31/17
4. Implement new annual performance evaluation program by 3/31/17
5. Implement web-based HR benefit information portal for associates by 1/1/17

Information Technology

1. Achieve Budget by 3/31/17

2. Implement approved IT maximization plan based on Prelude report by 1/1/17
3. Develop and implement resident and associate portals for information sharing and HR benefit reports for employees by 1/1/17
4. Maximize Matrix Care EMR training and implementation by 11/1/16

APPENDIX C
LEADERSHIP VALUES WORKSHEET

1. Who do you admire as a manager/leader and why?
2. What management books have you read?
3. What principles have you read that you have incorporated or would like to incorporate into your management style?
4. What is your life purpose, life mission, or life vision statement?
5. What are the current management principles you use in the areas of:
    - Planning and strategic planning
    - Organization and organizational charts
    - Job descriptions
    - Hiring
    - Orienting/training staff
    - Supervising
    - Making decisions
    - Solving problems
    - Expectations of line staff, peers, supervisors, vendors, and customers

- Customer service
- Building a team in your department
- Building employee morale
- Budgeting
- Staffing
- Managing/monitoring the budget
- Goal setting
- Monitoring key success factors of your department
- Monitoring staff and staff morale
- Employee evaluations
- Terminating employees
- Your professional development and education

6. Word pictures or illustrations that help to represent your principles.
7. What is your professional mission statement?
8. How can you use this exercise to improve your management skills and operations in the future?

APPENDIX D

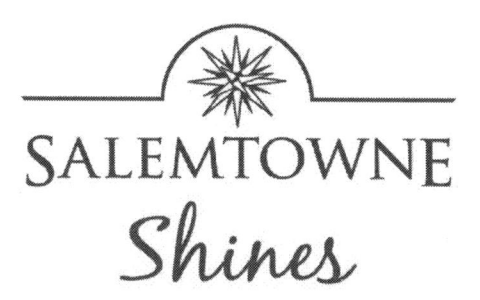

SALEMTOWNE Shines

Definition

Salemtowne Shines is the attitude, behavior and standards that enable us to provide exceptional service and positive experiences to those we work with, care for, and serve.

Salemtowne Mission Statement

Salemtowne is a nonprofit, continuing care retirement community that promotes the well-being of its residents by providing a caring environment.

Salemtowne is an ecumenical community that reflects the Moravian values of individual respect, hospitality, lifelong learning, and love of the arts.

The Salemtowne Motto

We are exceptional individuals providing exceptional care and services.

Foundation of Service

Greet everyone with a smile.

Anticipate, acknowledge, and act.

Be warm and genuine.

Our Promise to Team Members

At Salemtowne, our team members are the most important asset in providing exceptional care and service.

By promoting compassion, creativity, positive attitude, respect, and teamwork, we encourage individual growth and maximum potential. Salemtowne supports a work environment where diversity is embraced and family is valued, where every life shines.

14 Commitments

1. I create one-of-a-kind positive experiences for those we serve.
2. I own every problem I see.
3. I build meaningful relationships with those I work with and serve.
4. I present a professional image through dress, behavior, and communication.
5. I protect information and assets of those we work with and serve.
6. I create an exceptional environment that is safe, secure, and inviting.

7. I am truthful in what I say and honest in what I do.
8. I provide valued service and consistent quality.
9. I seek opportunities to learn and develop new skills.
10. I contribute to a team atmosphere of respect and mutual support.
11. I am welcoming and warm to everyone who explores our community and services.
12. I look for the good in others and trust their positive intentions.
13. I promptly respond to the needs and expressed wishes of those we care for and serve.
14. I understand, accept, and embrace my role in Salemtowne, our values, and mission statement.

APPENDIX E

BS&A PROPOSAL TO BUILD (FILL IN THE BLANK)

The Plan

BS&A would work with Management, the Board, Residents, and the Consultants (defined below) (together the "Project Development Team" - PDT) to prepare the Plan for the Community that would define key elements of the Project including, but not limited to unit mix, pricing, programs, operating expense structure, construction and other project costs and the financing structure (both pre-finance and permanent financing). It will include information from the Project Development Team regarding the market, master site plan, design, operating assumptions, construction cost, and timeline assumptions as well as marketing tactics for the Project. Finally, the Plan would provide a timeline for the completion of the work.

- The primary tasks involved in completing the Plan include:
- Completing a Market Analysis.
- Designing a Site Plan, Developing an Architectural Program (i.e. square feet) and Completing a Conceptual Design Package.
- Developing Project Costs.
- Creating Operating Projections.

- Establishing a Financing Structure.
- Risks and Risk Mitigation Strategies; and
- Confirming a Timeline and Next Steps.

Setting the Stage: Selecting Planning Team, Completing a Market Analysis, and Refining the Existing Financial Projections

Estimated Time: 8–12 Weeks

Selecting the Project Team

BS&A would work with Management and the Board (Repositioning Task Force) to assemble team members needed to complete the Plan including drafting and coordinating requests for proposal ("RFPs") and assisting in negotiating contracts. BS&A would work with Management in determining other team members (the "Consultants") which would extend the skill sets of the Management team. In addition to the Consultants, we would recommend that the PDT (as defined below) include several residents of the Community, a wide range of the management team of the Community and several Board members. In total we would recommend that the PDT consist of approximately 20 people.

Consultants to identify, interview and with which to contract would include:

- An architect ("the Architect") for leading the site plan analyses, completing a conceptual design package and a high-level square foot program analysis.
- A construction manager ("the Construction Manager") to create construction estimates.
- A market analysis firm ("the Market Analyst") to prepare a full

market analysis for use in determining the scope of the project.
- An interior design firm ("the Interior Designer") for developing finish levels and furniture, fixture and equipment estimates associated with the project; and
- A civil engineering firm ("the Civil Engineer") to help with identifying any design and zoning issues.

BS&A would have a call with the Management team and Board (Repositioning Task Force) to understand the key criteria that are important to them and would then establish an RFP, recommend potential firms to contact, lead the evaluation of the responses with the team to the RFP and assist the team in the negotiation of the contracts with the Consultants. Typically, this process will take four to six weeks depending on the availability of the team for any required interviews with the potential Consultants. This activity can be phased as the first firm required is the Market Analyst.

While these consultants may ultimately be involved in the development of the Project should it go forward, BS&A would work with Management to ensure that the initial contracts be structured with the Consultants to provide ONLY consultative services for completing the Plan. *The Community will **not** be required to engage them for the execution of the Plan. It is anticipated that each of these Consultants will contract directly with Salemtowne, and that BS&A will not be responsible for the performance of their services as provided for within their contract with Salemtowne.*

Completing a Market Analysis

The market analysis would be completed in parallel with the selection of the other consultants. The market analysis would include:

- Defining the primary market area ("PMA") for the Community (the area from which a substantial number of the residents are anticipated to originate).
- Gathering demographic information about the PMA including age, income, marital status, and other pertinent information.
- Understanding housing values based on available information including pricing trends, days on market, and analyzing values by different price points and age of homes in the PMA.
- Completing a competitive analysis on independent living, assisted living and memory support facilities including occupancy, pricing, programs offered, geographic area from which they draw, difficult units to sell, expansion/repositioning plans and other anecdotal information. It is anticipated that this data will be collected through industry sources, phone calls and on-site visits to significant competition and other knowledgeable market resources. In addition, they should contact government agencies, investment bankers, and other industry professionals to identify any planned projects for the PMA.
- Comparing and contrasting the Community's existing units across the continuum to those of the competition with a focus on where you have a competitive advantage with considering the pricing and programs of your existing units as well as allowing for

the scope of the Project to compliment your existing units; and
- Preparing penetration rates and demand analyses for each level of care based on the information gathered above.

BS&A would supervise the activity of the Marketing Analyst to be certain that they are completing the scope of work required and in the time frame identified.

Based on the information gathered in the market analysis, we would work with the PDT to develop a recommended scope for the Community including:

- Number of units by level of care.
- Mix of units by unit size.
- Pricing units by level of care.
- Programs and services to be offered; and
- Any recommended NEW independent living units would also consider your current mix of units to not duplicate product that is already in place!

Preparing Financial Projections

During this time frame, BS&A would also work with the Community to create a baseline financial projection, most likely based on your fiscal year FY 2021 budget and adjusted for any ongoing capital needs as well as operational changes related to the new project. This financial projection will serve as the baseline analysis against which to compare the outcome of the Plan and understand how the Plan is financially accretive for the Community. It will also help us understand any existing debt capacity of the Community.

Preparing the Business Plan

Estimated Time: 8 – 12 Weeks

Upon completion of the market analysis and scope recommendations, we would recommend that we bring a project development team ("the PDT") together 1 1/2 days to discuss and review potential site solutions that meet the recommended scope for the Project ("the Planning Session").

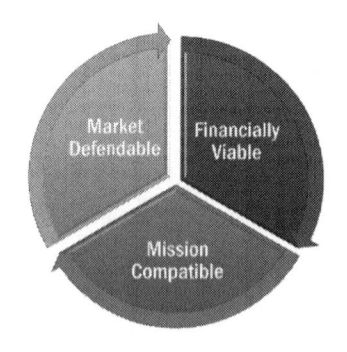

We would prepare a summary of the material that has been completed to date and have the PDT review it ahead of this meeting. A potential agenda for the meeting would include:

1. Day 1
    a. Confirm objectives for the Plan – Management and BS&A
    b. Discuss status of the Community - Management
    c. Understand key points from the Market Analysis – Marketing Consultant, Management and BS&A
    d. BREAK
    e. Confirm potential Project scope – All
    f. Understand baseline financial projections – Management with BS&A support
    g. LUNCH
    h. Early afternoon

           i. Design and construction team work on potential site solutions for the Project based on scope above
           ii. Finance and marketing team work on high level financial analysis based on scope above
        i. Evening
           i. Full team comes back together to review
              1. Site analysis
              2. High level financial analysis
2. Day 2
    a. Update site analysis
    b. Update high level financial analysis for repositioning of existing campus or development of new campus
    c. Confirm selected site plan
    d. Develop timeline for completing the Plan

<u>**We would work with the team and the Consultants to further refine this agenda to make the best use of the team's time!**</u>

Design and Construction Analysis

After completion of the Planning Session, BS&A would work with the PDT in refining a conceptual plan for the Project. This Plan would include refining the site plan from the Planning Session and providing conceptual drawings for the Project and a program (i.e., square feet by type of construction/use) in order to assist in the estimate of the construction costs associated with the selected initiative.

Based on the scope defined in the Plan, BS&A and Management would work with the Architect, the Civil Engineer, and the Interior Design Firm to confirm basic conceptual parameters for the Project including:

- Site plan.
- Number of stories planned.
- Expected design/skin materials.
- General unit layout based on the proposed unit mix.
- Definition of common spaces.
- Interior design finish levels.
- FF&E high level budget.
- Parking plan.
- Project square feet; and
- Understanding how the Project could impact existing facilities and operations such as dining.

Upon completion of the conceptual design, we would work with the Construction manager to estimate:

- Initial high-level construction cost estimates.
- Assistance in identifying the construction timeline including regulatory and zoning approval process; and

We would also work with the PDT to estimate other project costs (design costs, FFE, owner supplied equipment, low voltage, marketing costs, other consultant costs, legal costs, contingencies, etc.).

The Civil Engineer would also be involved in this process to assist with requirements likely to be established by the local government, and to understand timelines associated with the development of the Project. Typically, this element of the Plan would include initial estimates of development and construction timelines and fees associated with the Project during the pre-permanent finance timeframe as well as after permanent financing so it is clear what type of pre-finance capital would be required to reach permanent financing and how long it would take.

Marketing Plan

One of the characteristics of a successful business plan is to identify those characteristics that would distinguish this Project from other potentially competitive communities. What are the needs in the market? How do you want to create a demonstrable advantage – in effect jump the market? How do you leverage the existing strengths of your community?

The Marketing Plan should include items associated with the Plan including marketing timeline for pre-finance, construction and fill up activities related to the Project, confirmation of number of units, mix of units and pricing for units as well as programs associated with those units:

- Staffing.
- Budget.
- Advertising and promotion focus.
- Expected timelines for priority campaign, 10% presales campaign and fill up; and
- Key issues.

We would work with the marketing team to establish the outline for the plan, review drafts that they prepare and make recommendations for additions to the marketing plan.

Financial Analysis

BS&A would complete a 10-year cash flow (non- GAAP) financial projection for the Project. BS&A would ascertain how the Project would be accretive to the financial results of the Community and demonstrate financial viability for the future. The assumptions for the financial projection will be based on the scope as developed by the PDT as well as the actual performance of Salemtowne and will include:

- Revenue
    - Number of units by level of care.
    - Pricing of units (entrance fees and monthly service fees).
    - Fill up of units.
    - Attrition from the independent living and utilization of health care based on historical data or an actuarial study; and
    - Other revenue.
- Expenses (incremental to the existing Community)
    - Staffing (by department by position by year).
    - Wage rates.
    - Benefit structure.
    - Non-labor expenses including:
        - Supplies.
        - Meal costs.
        - Insurance.
        - Utilities; and
        - Property taxes.
- Project Costs (including estimates from the construction manager)

- Architectural and engineering costs.
- Construction costs (including escalation assumptions, contingencies, and contractor fees).
- Furniture fixtures and equipment (including any low voltage and technology needs).
- Appropriate contingencies.
- Marketing costs; and
- Legal and financing costs.
▷ Financing Structure
  - Initial pre-finance capital required.
    - Sources and rates.
  - Permanent capital required.
    - Debt structure (temporary versus permanent).
    - Interest rates.
    - Funded interest; and
    - Reserves.
▷ Timeline; and
  - Construction timing; and
  - Fill up timing.
▷ Impact on the Community.

It is anticipated that the Plan, beyond the baseline financial analysis, will require one initial financial projection and one update as the team works through changes in the Project for the Plan. Two sensitivity analyses will also be completed to help us to understand the Project's financial performance based on different occupancy levels and operating margins. Any additional financial analyses would require additional professional fees to complete.

Timeline and Next Steps—the Plan will also include documentation of the timeline associated with executing the Project, key risks and rewards associated with the Project (and risk mitigation strategies) and recommended next steps.

Communication Plan

To ensure timely and ongoing communication with Management and the PDT throughout the process, BS&A would propose the following meeting schedule and typical agenda topics listed below:

- Kick off Meeting/Planning Session – Defining the Project Scope and Developing Site Solutions (two-day meeting described above):
- Project Development Team ("PDT") Meetings (usually twice a month throughout the Plan process – one in person and one by phone):
  - Review and confirm Project scope and key assumptions.
  - Review information from the Marketing Plan.
  - Review assumptions for the Project's financial projections.
  - Confirm the timeline for financial projections to be completed and items required from team members.
  - Review design, construction, and civil information including:
    - Site plan,
    - Building layouts,

- Common spaces review, and
- Initial construction costs as prepared by the Contractor.
  - Review of initial and updated financial projections; and
  - Review of drafts and final Business Plan.
- *Management Meetings*—Meet with Board and Management, as required, at the conclusion of the engagement to present the findings from the Business Planning process. We are also glad to include a meeting with community residents to discuss the Plan.

Deliverable

The deliverable for the Plan would be a bullet style Power Point document summarizing all the information prepared above, including a project timeline, and recommended next steps. The financial projections would be based on information available at the time of the development of the Plan and would be updated throughout the development process as assumptions are likely to change based on gaining more information and time elapsed. The deliverable would also include a section on potential risks associated with the Project and suggestions as to how to mitigate those risks.

Timing

The ultimate timing of the Plan would be determined through the planning process with the Management and Board and based on outcome and completion of the various components of the Business Plan. The typical time frame for completion of the Plan, as described in this document is 5 to 6 months, depending on your availability.

Professional Fees

Most business plans we lead cost between $85,000 and $100,000, in 2023 dollars. The timing of the payment of the professional fees associated are outlined in the below table:

SERVICE	FEES
Upon Signing of the Engagement Letter	
Upon Completion of the Market Analysis	
Upon Completion of the Planning Session	
Upon Completion of First Draft of the Financial Projections	
Upon Finalization of the Financial Projections	
Upon Completion of the Draft Plan	
Total	

Also, the professional fees referenced above do not include other Consultants fees.

Services included in the above estimate:
- Development of RFPs and interviews of consultants.
- Conference calls and meetings with the Project Development Team, Management and Board as described above.
- Facilitation of the Plan.
- Development of Financial Projections; and
- Preparation of the deliverable

ABOUT THE AUTHOR

Mark Steele has been an innovator in the senior living field for more than 35 years. His extensive background in leadership development, repositioning, and change management has benefitted multiple communities and prepared leaders to take the next steps in their careers. Across his years of service, Mark was a nursing home administrator, an executive director, a regional vice president managing five communities, a president of China operations, and president and CEO of a single-site life plan community. He has consulted and spoken publicly about the need to change models of caring for older adults nationally and internationally.

Mark is passionate about mentoring leaders. He has a doctorate degree in leadership and global perspectives from George Fox University and an MBA degree from LaVerne University. He is a certified executive coach and a certified nonprofit board consultant. With his wife, Cindy, he leads The Steele Consulting Group, which empowers boards and develops leaders to become their best and navigate life stage transitions. (thesteeleconsultinggroup.com)

Mark loves to spend time with family, camping, traveling, hiking, biking, mountain climbing and reading. He and Cindy currently live near Nashville, Tennessee.

REFRESH, RENEW & REPOSITION

Made in the USA
Columbia, SC
21 March 2025